Beaux's Tale

A Blue Heeler with Wanderlust

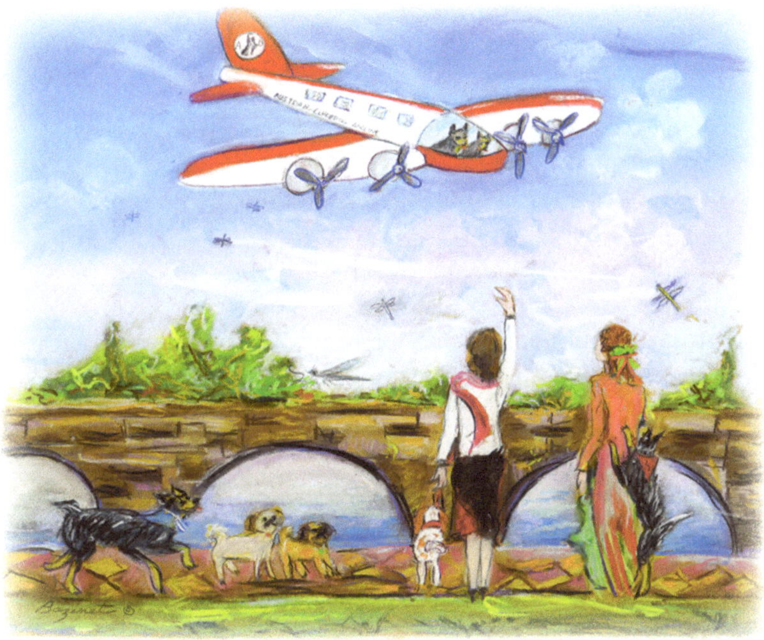

Written and Painted by

Jane Bazinet

the Peppertree Press
Sarasota, Florida

Graphic design by Rebecca Barbier.

For information regarding permission,
call 941-922-2662 or contact us at our website:
www.peppertreepublishing.com or write to:
the Peppertree Press, LLC.
Attention: Publisher
1269 First Street, Suite 7
Sarasota, Florida 34236

ISBN: 978-1-61493-542-1

Library of Congress Number: 2016918962

Printed July 2017

Lyrical Romanticism

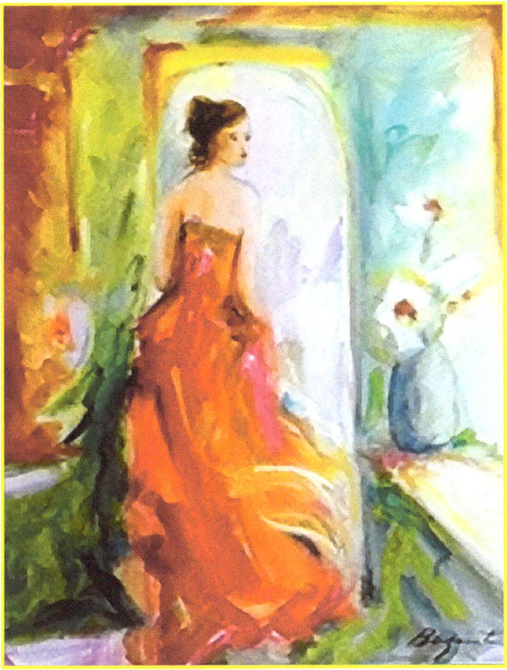

Jane Bazinet, has finally freed herself of her obligation to explain her art to anyone. The Louisiana native whose style is described as dwelling "at mysterious crossroads between poetic realism and abstract expressionism," makes a visual statement about people with romantic personalities.

"I love music, dance, opera and ballet. I was raised in the French Cajun area of Louisiana where everybody learns to dance early." This love is palpably evident in many of her pieces.

Her lyrical, figurative work tends to mirror her own disposition, her thoughts, her feelings. Taking time to enjoy life, she paints calm and relaxed scenes containing quiet, pensive, elongated figures, whose poses and surrounding suggest none of the panic or anxiety that often accompany logical, rational analysis. Her people are simply engaged in the "lost art of thinking."

Painting the human form in pigments on canvas may be risky, but successful endeavors are magical. We experience a resonance combining painter, viewer, and subject: intangible ... esoteric ... and real. And, in that way, our stories are all related.

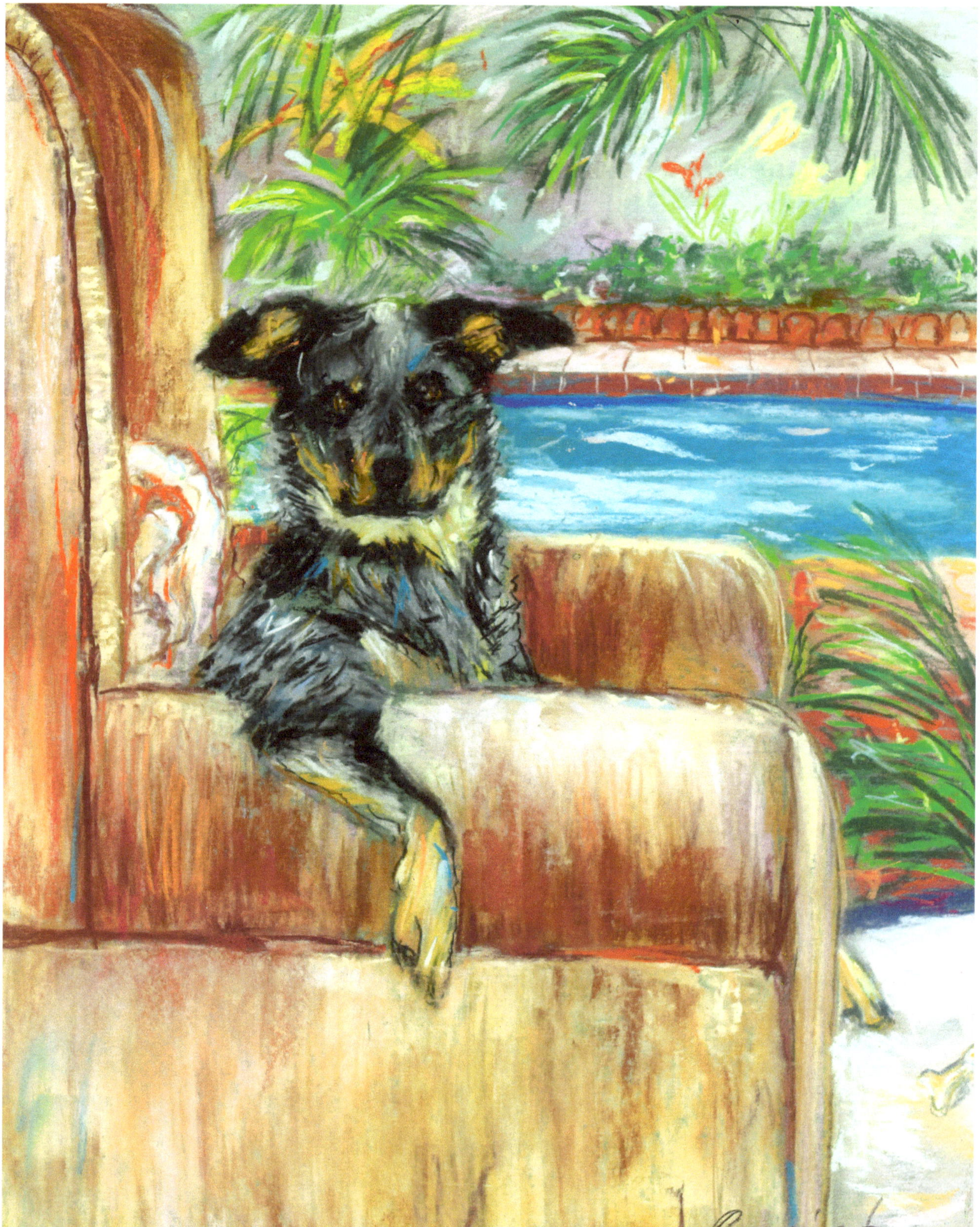

Beaux was my first dog

The story actually started at Art Expo in New York. The publisher of Printworld Encyclopedia was discussing what images of my art we should use in a certain book. Out of nowhere she asked me to call her psychic in Chadsford, Pennsylvania, a place I had thought of moving to. I found this a little bizzare, but I called the psychic ready to discuss my art and my life as an artist. Instead her first word were, "what is it with you and the dog?" I recall saying, "I have no dog. I don't really relate to dogs and they smell funny. I have a cat. A very smart Tonkinese." This cat went everywhere with me. He loved his leash walks and long car trips.

Soon thereafter, I travelled to Oklahoma with my mother and a friend. While in Oklahoma, my mother and I visited the "Phillips Ranch." When we entered the gate (pay station), a weird-looking, gray and tan, wolf-like animal stepped in front of the car. It had a daring look in his eyes until I paid the fee, then he stepped aside. Needless to say, I thought this is a very smart animal. I was intrigued and just a little in love. I stopped and praised it. "You are beautiful and one of the most intelligent beings I have ever met." It listened but did not let me near. Upon leaving the ranch, I found it waiting for me at the exit. I waved and could have sworn it waved back.

So, now I started asking everyone I meet about the gray and tan, wolf-like dog. "What is it?" Finally someone said, "Why, Jane, that's a dammed old cattle dog."

At the time I couldn't find much information about the breed, just a few photos. However as time went by I discovered it to be a Queensland heeler or an Australian cattle dog. A "blue heeler" is a dingo mix used for endurance and intelligence in the outback.

On Thanksgiving of that year, I flew out to Houston, Texas, to be with my daughter. My friend from Oklahoma, Jay, met me there. He asked me to go with him out to his car. "I have a problem," he said, as he opened the car door. Under a blanket was an infant blue heeler, which he presented to me as a gift! His name was registered as "Beausevis."

This baby flew back with me to Florida. I went straight to the vet. I renamed him "Beaux, the handsome one." The idea came from visiting Les Baux, France. Never having had a dog before, I raised him like a human baby. Rocking him and even making him homemade food. Maxwell, my cat, loved this dog and they became inseparable.

Of course, he became a traveling fool, who was loved by all that met him. He went to stores, parties and loved to dance. Basically, he tried whatever I did. Little did I know Beaux could sense evil. He started smelling and became aggressive toward certain people. It usually turned out they were "bad news." The word in the neighborhood was "Beaux knows."

When I went out of the country, Beaux couldn't go. I always felt guilty about this and when I returned, I would do a painting of the places I went with Beaux in the picture! The paintings started at the pet sitter, at home posing in a new chair, or playing with his animal friends.

Gradually, this blossomed into fantasy. Thus, I painted a story about Beaux and his desire to travel to foreign countries. We now have Bailey and she is part of our story. Another purpose was to have a family book. In the back of the book, I included pages of the paintings that one can color. The paintings were done in pastels. Pastels are my private world.

The first painting of Beaux was at home, posing as a gentleman, in my new chair.

The paintings progressed with Beaux playing with animal friends at the pet sitter. I hope you enjoy.

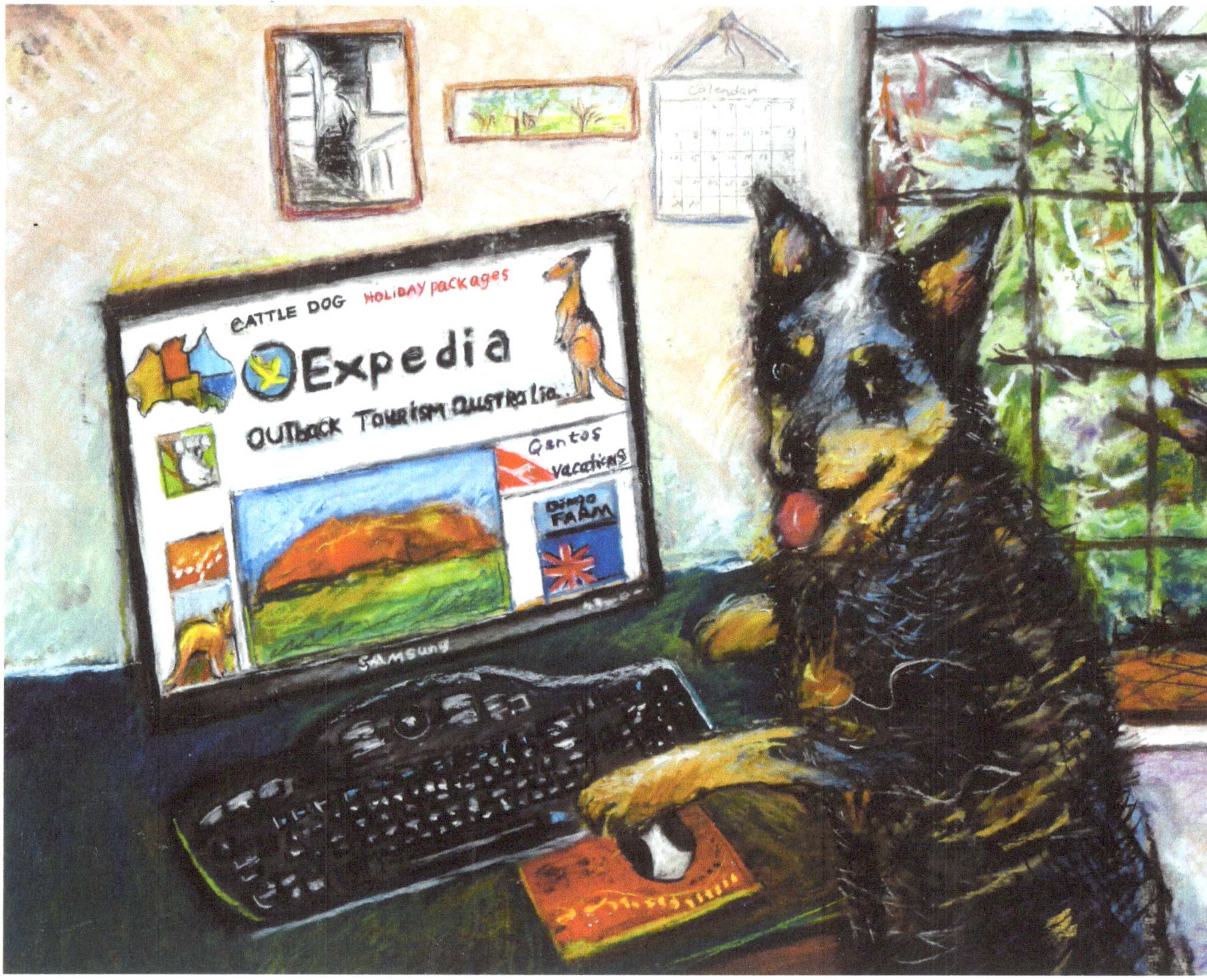

"Cattle Dog Holiday Packages"

Beaux's parents immigrated from Australia, but he was born in Austin, Texas. He spends most of his time with his human mom, Jane B. learning the ways of the world. Beaux dreams of the day he would visit his ancestral lands, but not quite yet.

Beaux devotes a lot of his spare time at the computer looking for "how to travel" information. His human mom is leaving for Europe, and he would certainly like a new adventure!

He decides to tag along and boards the plane with her. No pet sitter this time!

First stop, Paris, oh là là!

Our Travelers and Friends Have Names

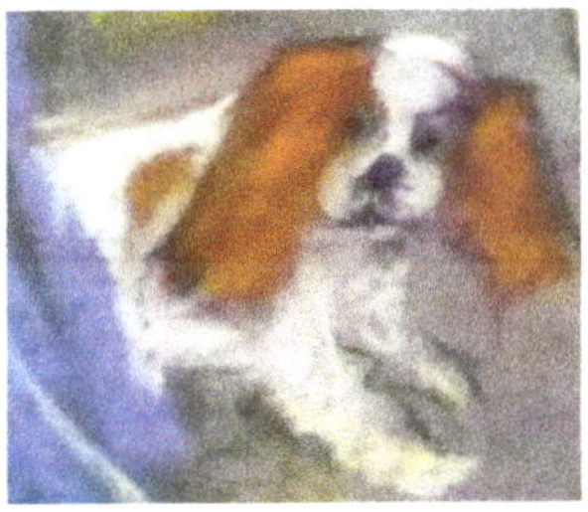
Lilly

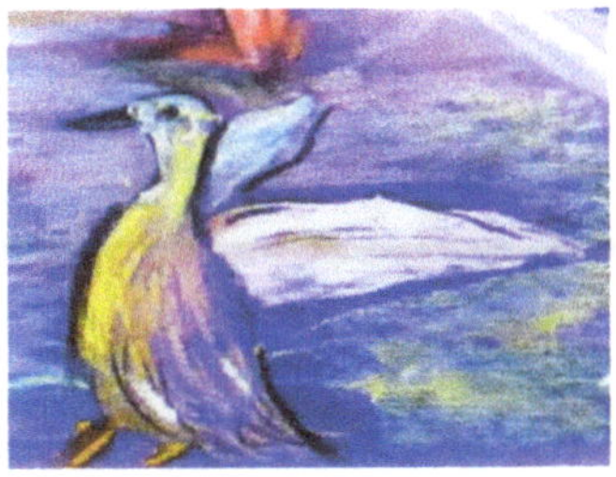
Emma

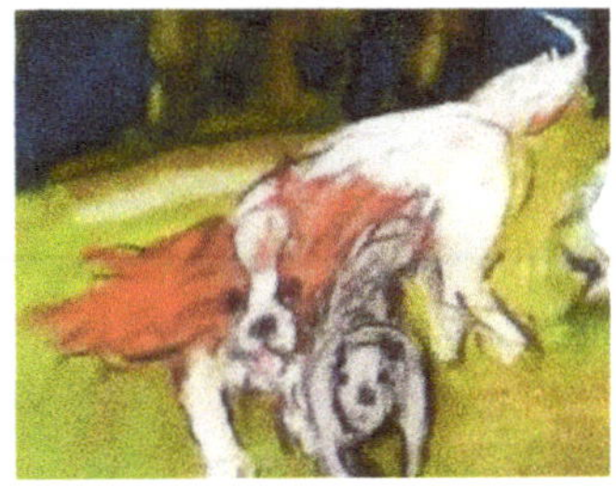
Squirrel & Birdie

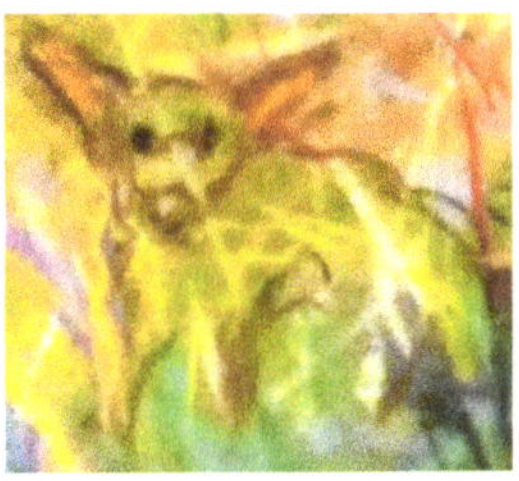
Desert Fox

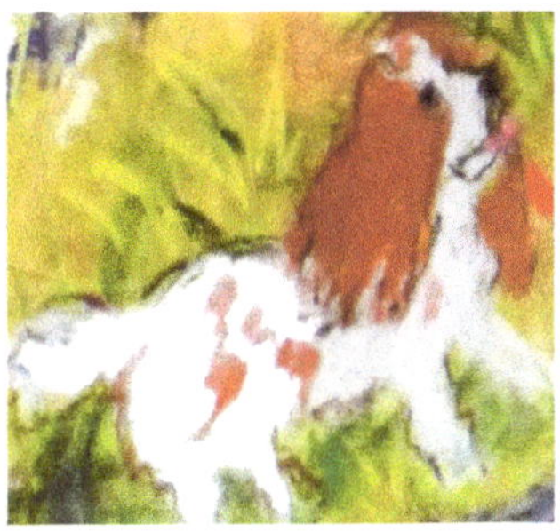
Reggie

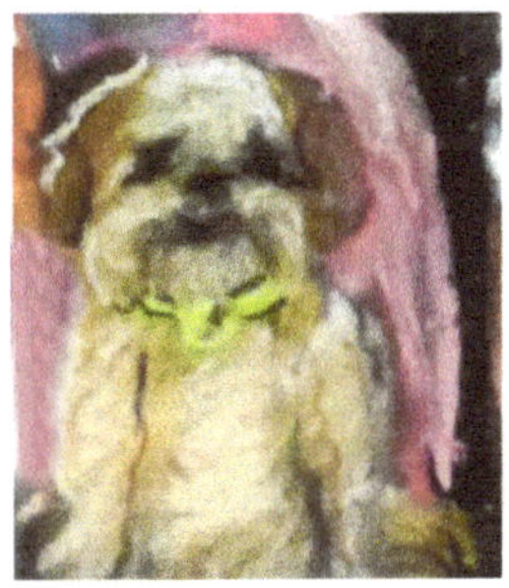
Heavenly

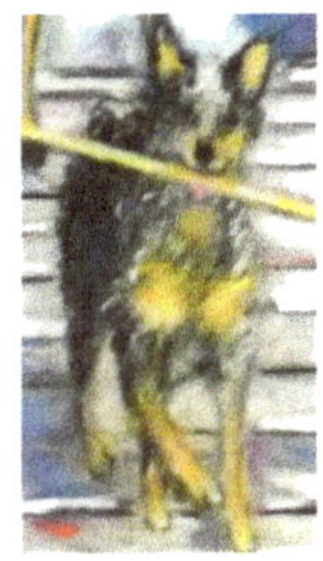
Beaux

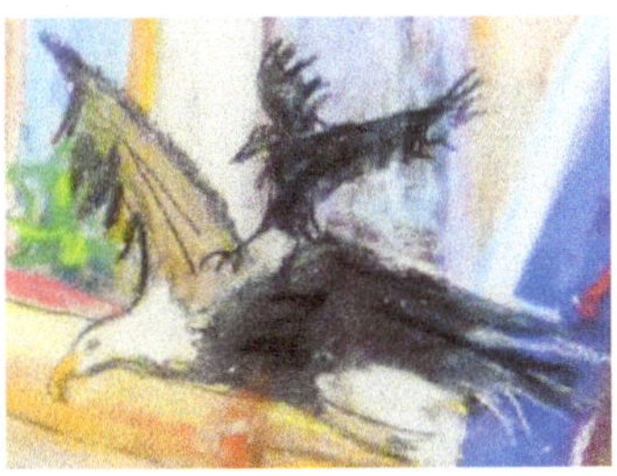
Arn and Corbin

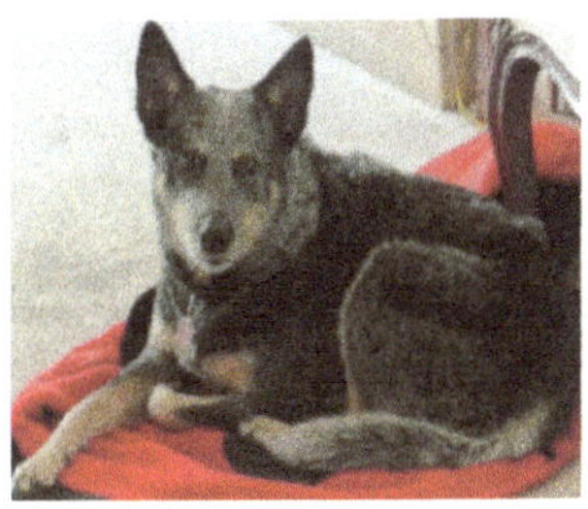
Bailey

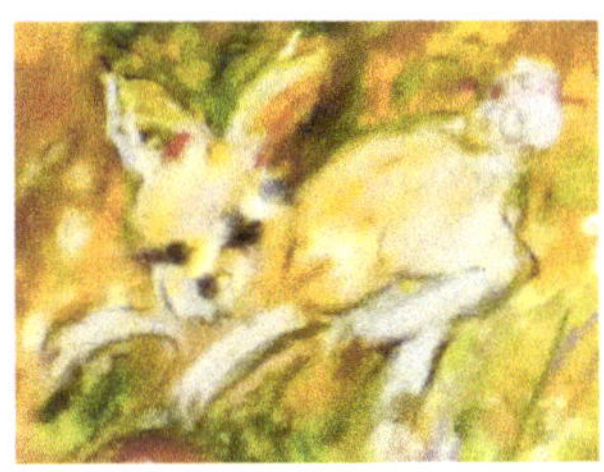
White Rabbit

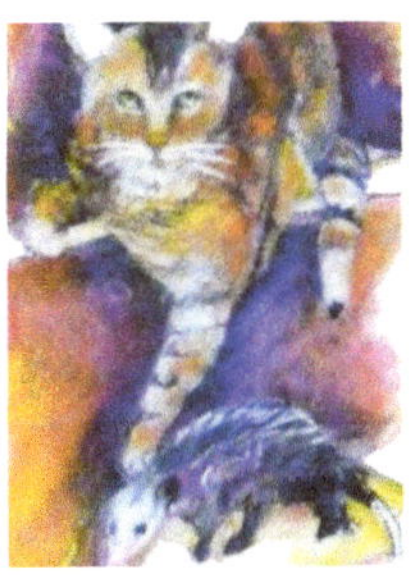
Kitty-Kitty

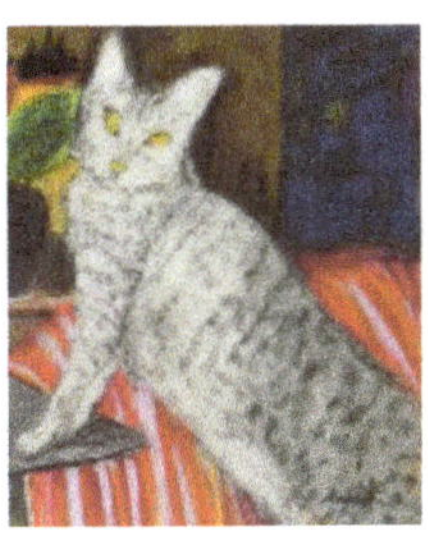
Prospedour

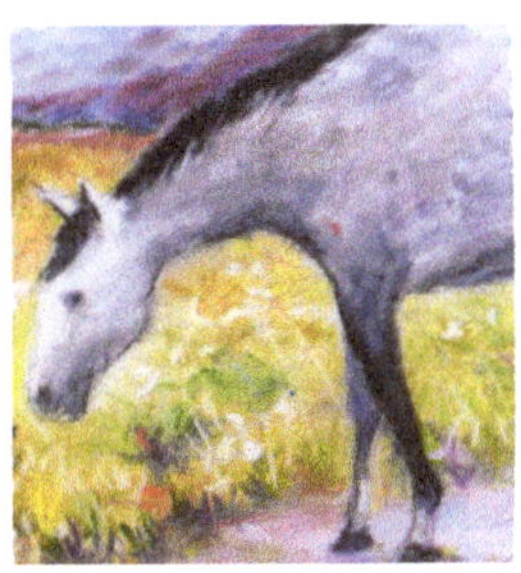
Jacques

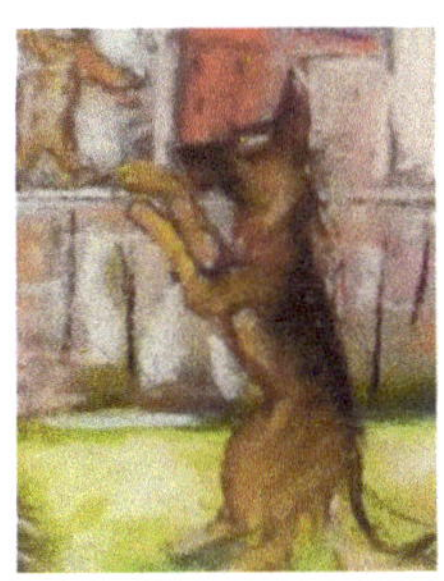
Minna

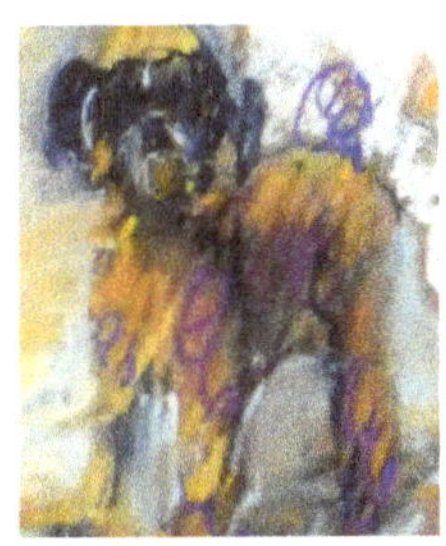
Chou-Chou

"Where's Her Head?"

On their first day in Paris, they visit the Louvre. Here Beaux sees "The Winged Victory," a marble sculpture of the Greek goddess, Nike. She has no head, yet there she stands in a prominent place at the museum! He realizes all things are possible.

Then and there, Beaux decides he will start a travel group for animals. He's sure they would all like to see and experience beautiful places in far-off lands.

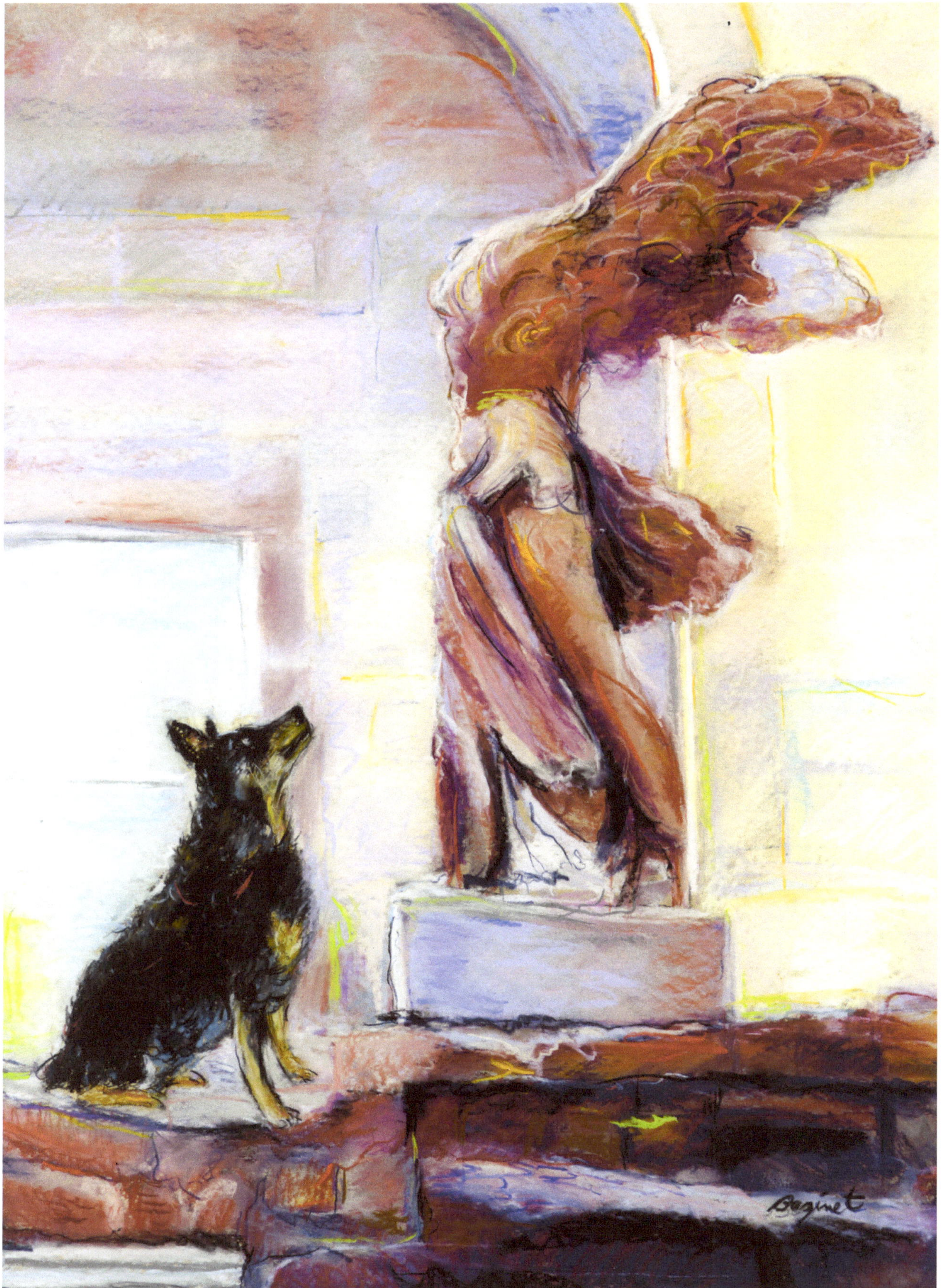

"Marché Jeanne d'Arc"

(outside Paris)

Beaux interviews animals at farmer's market, "Marché Jeanne d'Arc." All species are welcome, no prejudices with Beaux. Two cats sign up first, Kitty-Kitty and Prospedore. Here come three Cavaliers, Lilly, Bertie, and their son, Reggie. Chou-Chou and Heavenly are considering this trip also.

Rabbits, birds, even ducks and squirrels have signed on. In the distance Beaux spots a female Blue Heeler. "She's beautiful," he thinks, and she's alone! Unbeknownst to Beaux, she had already signed up for the trip.

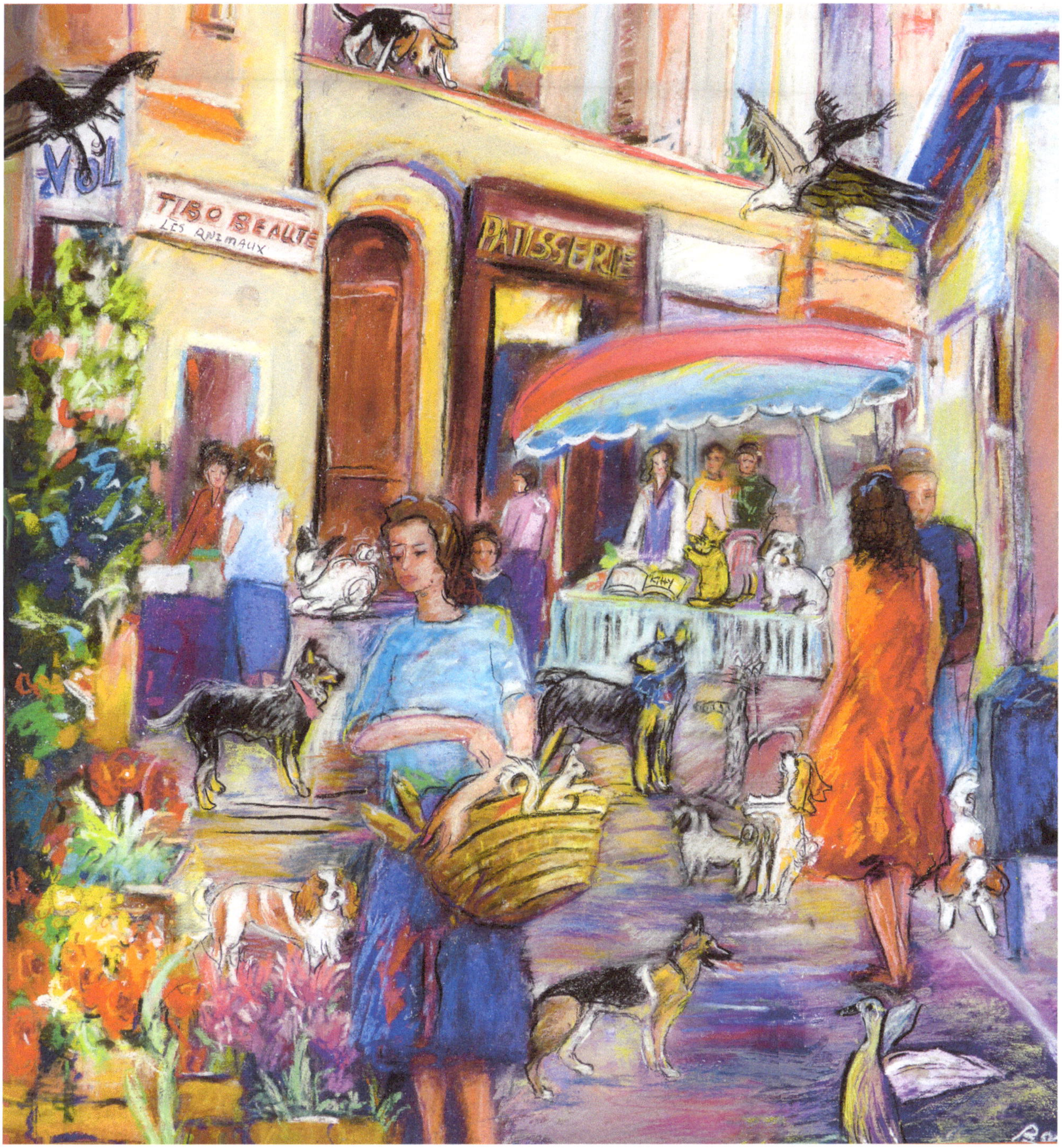
VOL
TIBO BEAUTE
LES ANIMAUX
PATISSERIE

"Châteaurenard"

(a town in France)

The group decides to stay at a Rooms To Let (Les Chambre d'Hôtes) Chez Jacqueline Sarrazi, a very good friend of Beaux's mom. Another good friend, Ms. Macdonald, is there with the Cavaliers, Lilly, Bertie, and Reggie.

Beaux feels a breeze, his senses detect the presence of that beautiful female blue heeler! Beaux finds out Bailey is her name. Their eyes meet, they could already tell this would be a life-long journey.

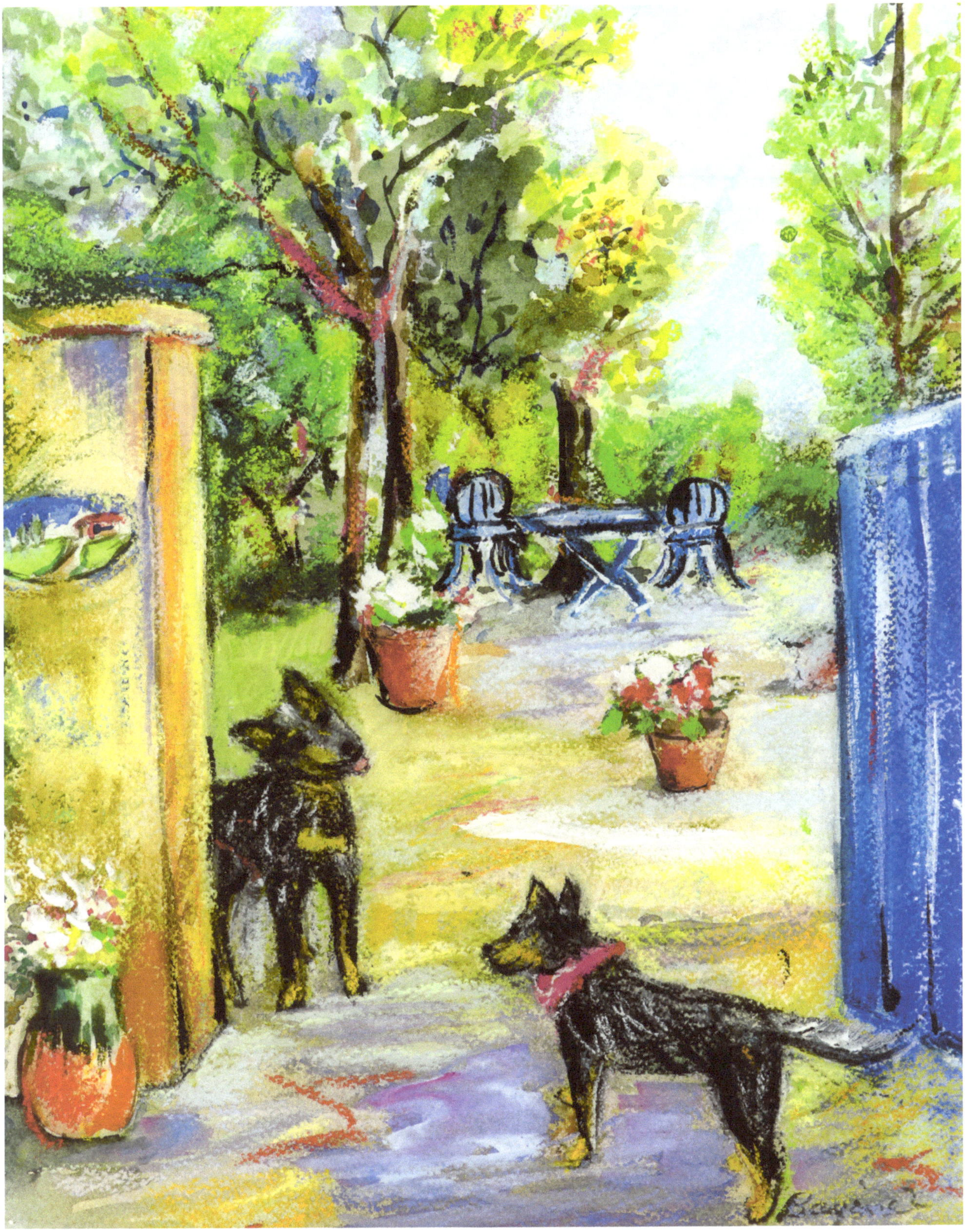

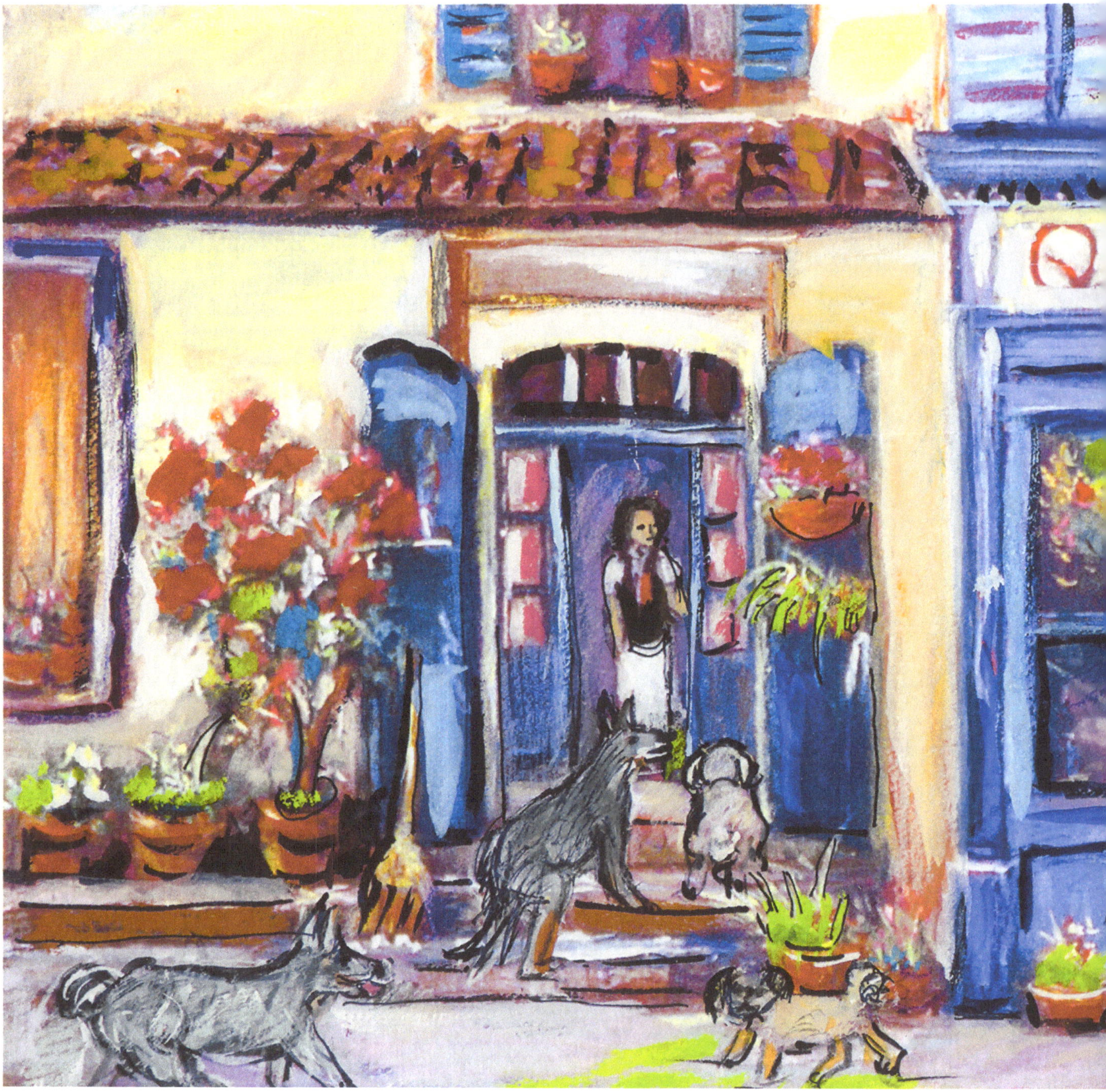

"Quincaillerie"

The group's journey begins in the town of Avignon. Located just outside is a village with a hardware store that also has food to go. They purchase a

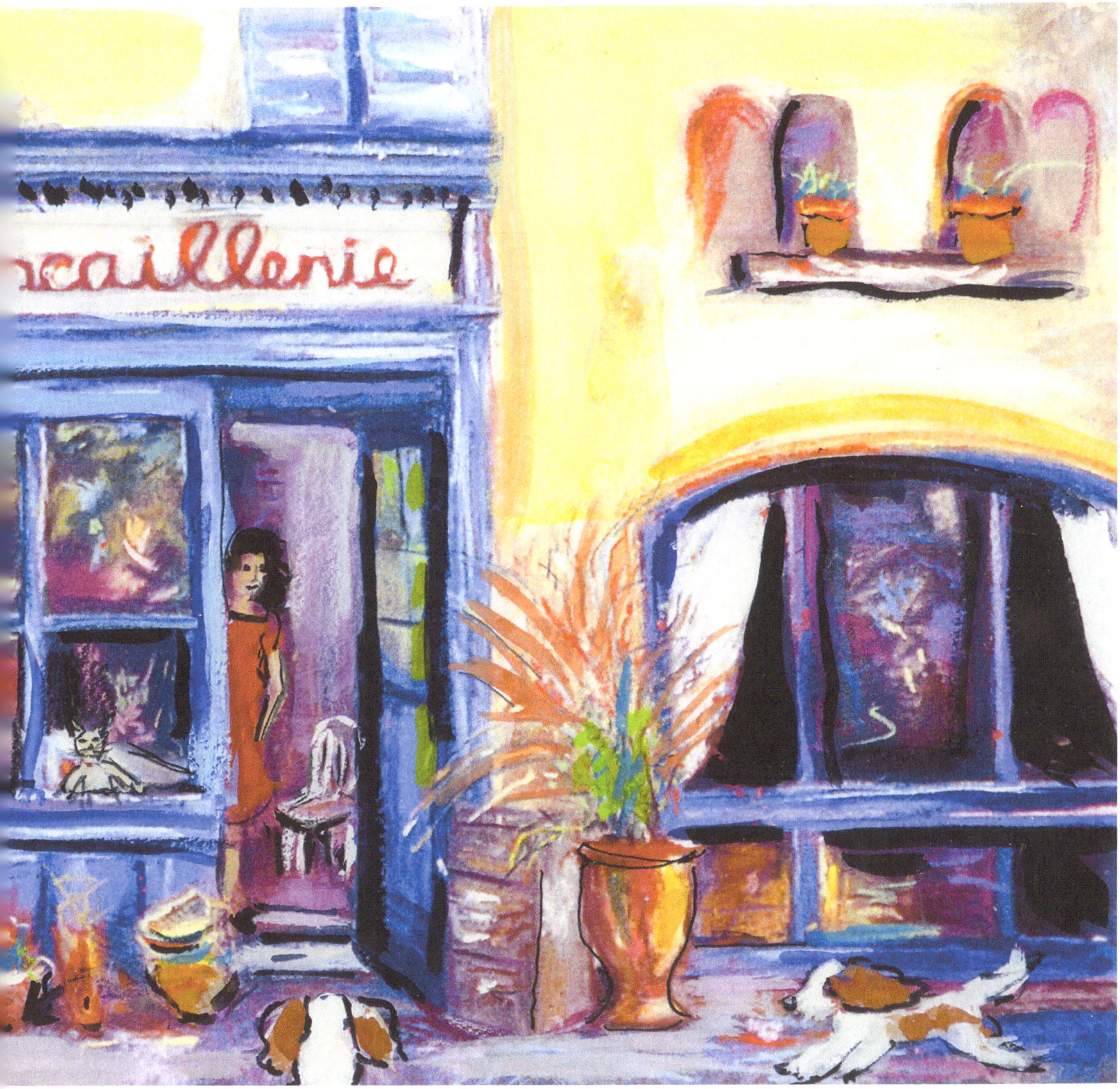

take-along lunch from the "Quincaillerie" of baguettes, apples, and an assortment of cheeses. Beaux also buys some sweets for a surprise later on. Chou-Chou and Heavenly are raring to go!

"La Camarque"

(protected area for animals in southern France)

Beaux has heard about le cheval (horse), "Jacques." He enlists Jacques to be their guide while traveling through La Camarque.

There is a rabbit and a desert fox, with big ears, waiting to join the expedition. Their group is really growing!

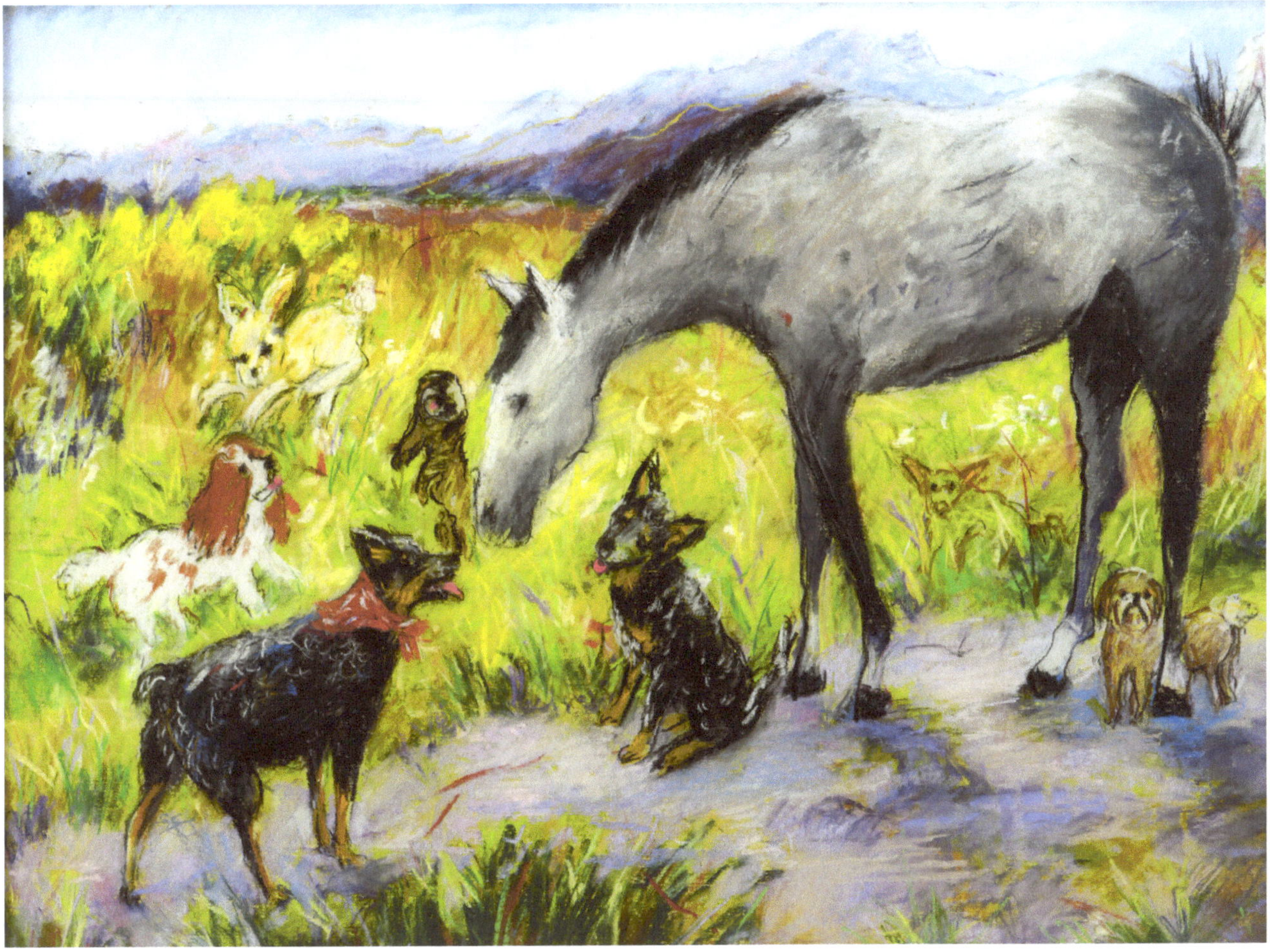

"Sunflower Fields"

It's a beautiful day. The sunflowers light up the fields throughout La Camarque.

Beaux weaves through the fields leading Jacques, to Bailey's delight. It's an exhausting hike, so Jacques gives a grateful Bertie a lift.

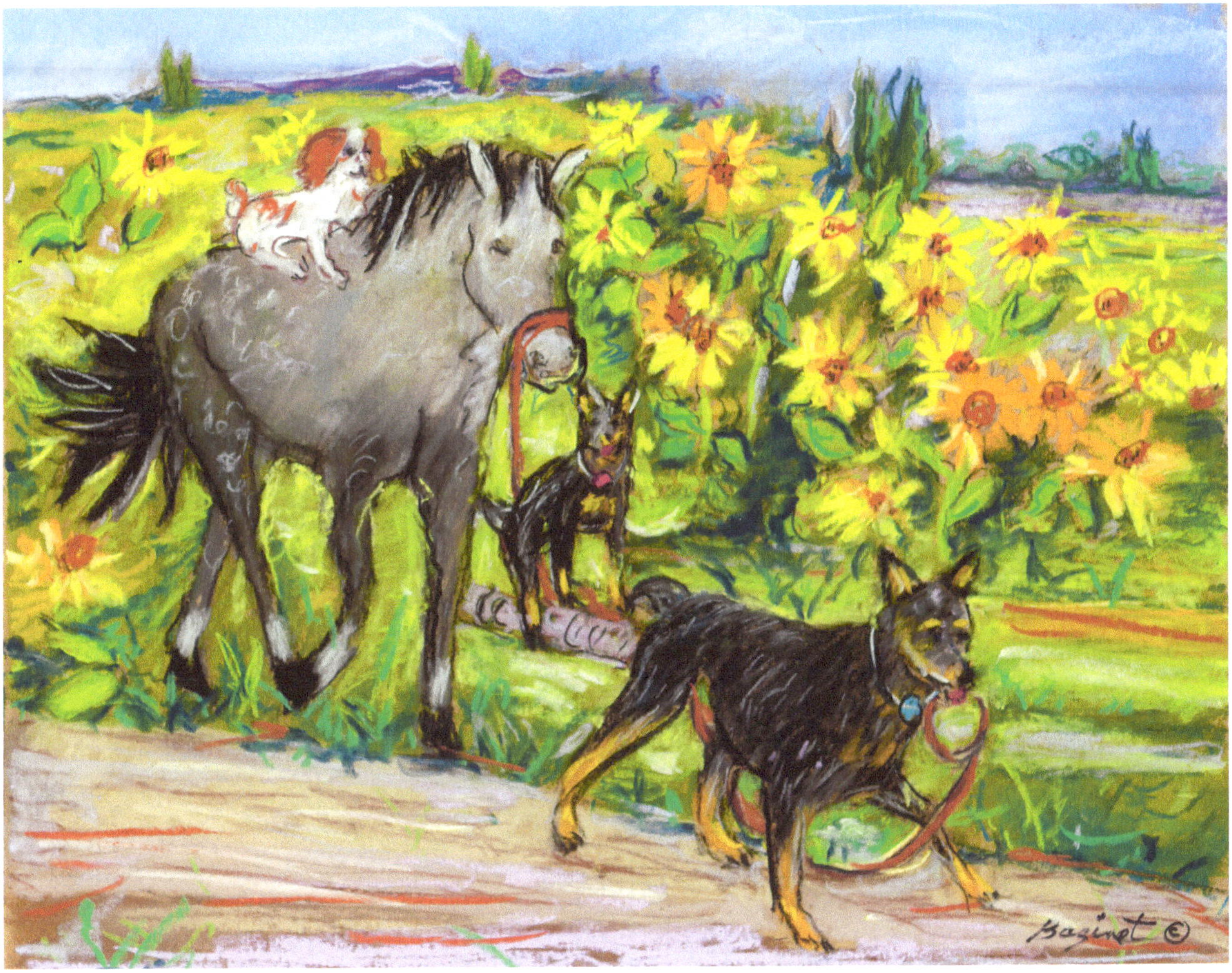

"Asissi"

Next, the group travels to Asissi, Italy, to visit the birthplace of St. Francis, the patron saint of animals. A local order of nuns have volunteered to act as tour guides.

The nuns bring along treats for the dogs in beautifully woven baskets. They all get so excited Beaux's herding instinct has to kick in trying to keep everyone together.

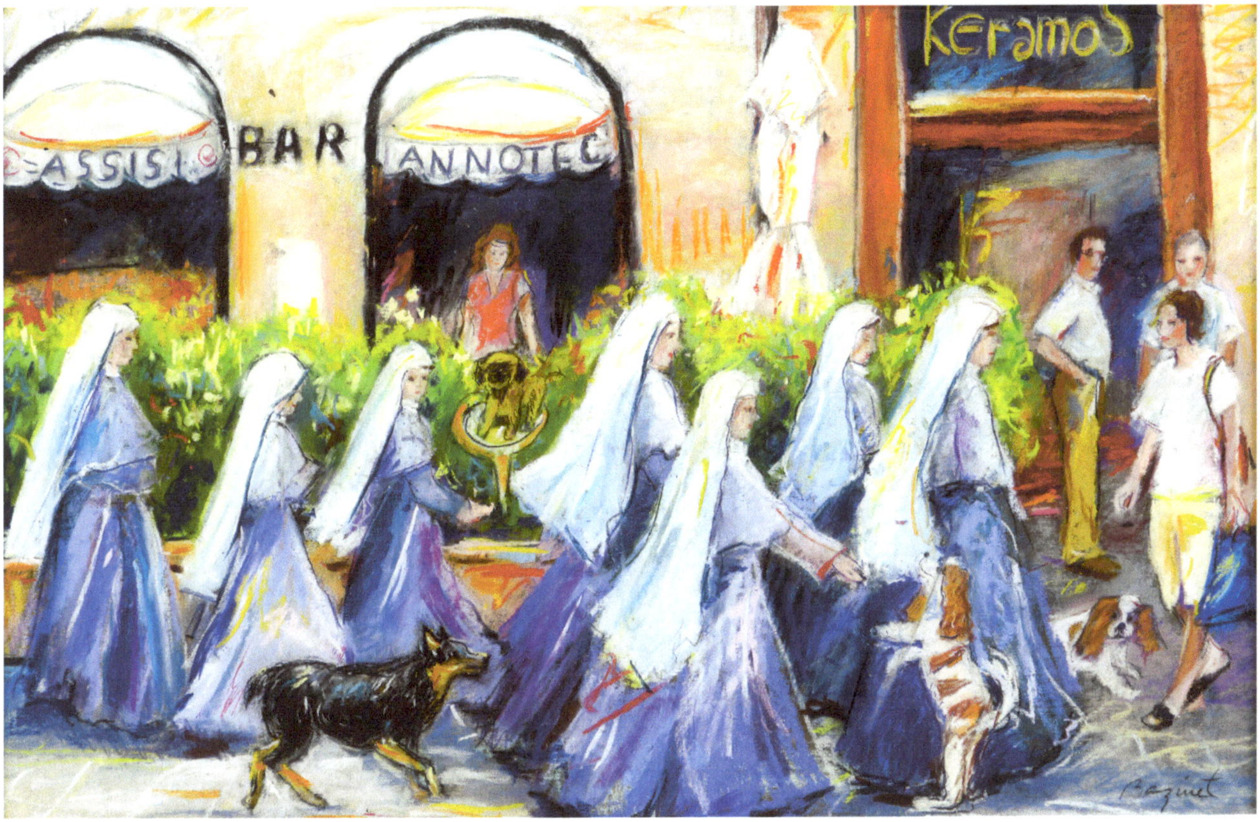
ASSISI
BAR
ANNOTEC
Keramos

"Biblos"

The tour is on it's way to Florence, Italy, where they hope to see "Pinocchio." They find a puppet store where animals are allowed. To their amazement, they spot Pinocchio inside. When Beaux gets a chance to meet with him, Pinocchio reveals he wants to be a real flesh and blood boy!

Beaux encourages Pinocchio, "If I can start a tour group, maybe your dream can come true."

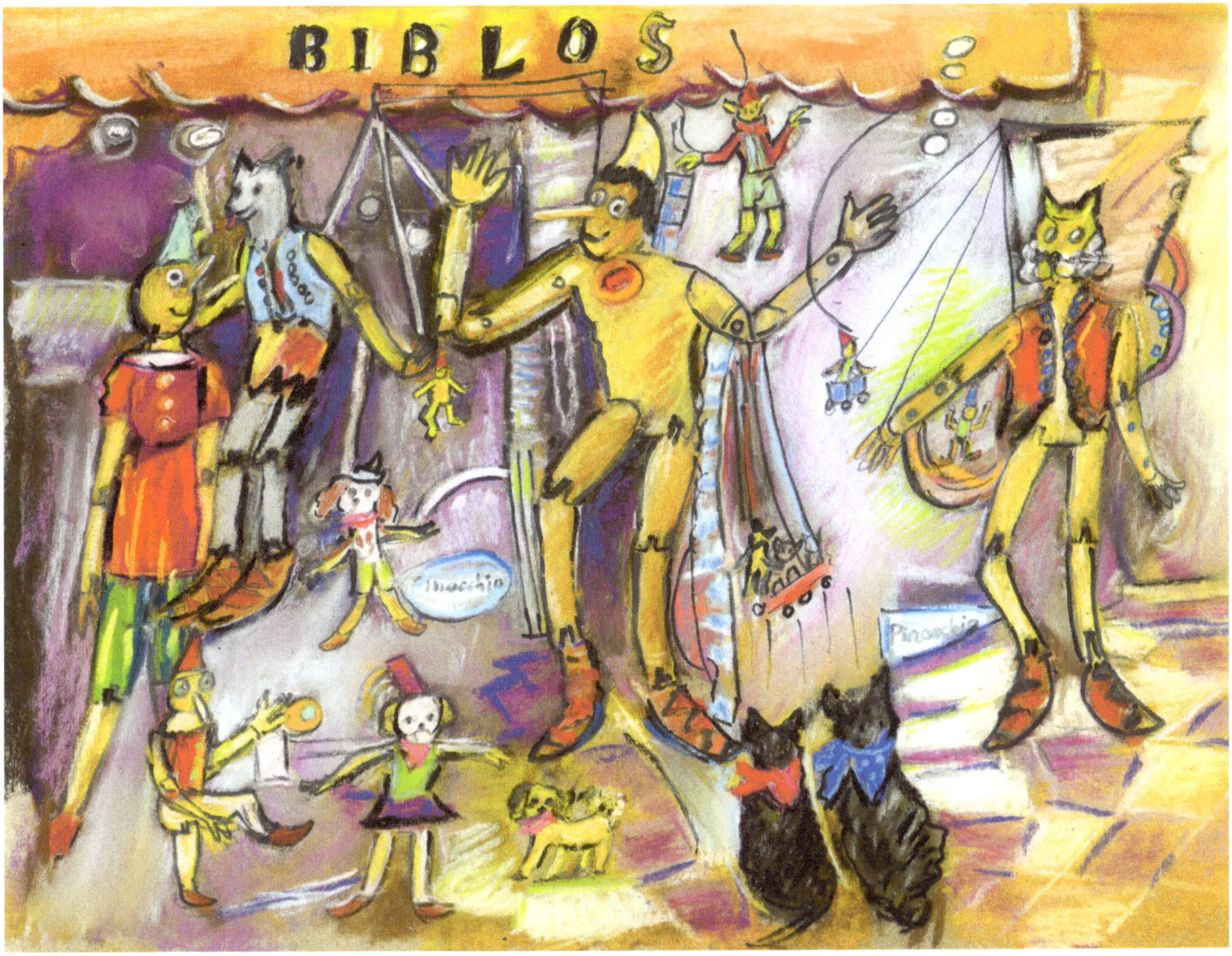
BIBLOS
Pinocchio

"The Vatican"

While visiting the Vatican with the tour group, they are taken by the colorful uniforms the Swiss Guards are wearing. Beaux sees a lance one of the Guards holds, "Aha, a stick—I must have it!"

He snatches the lance from the startled guard. Off they run—now they're in trouble. Beaux soon forgets his visit with the Pope.

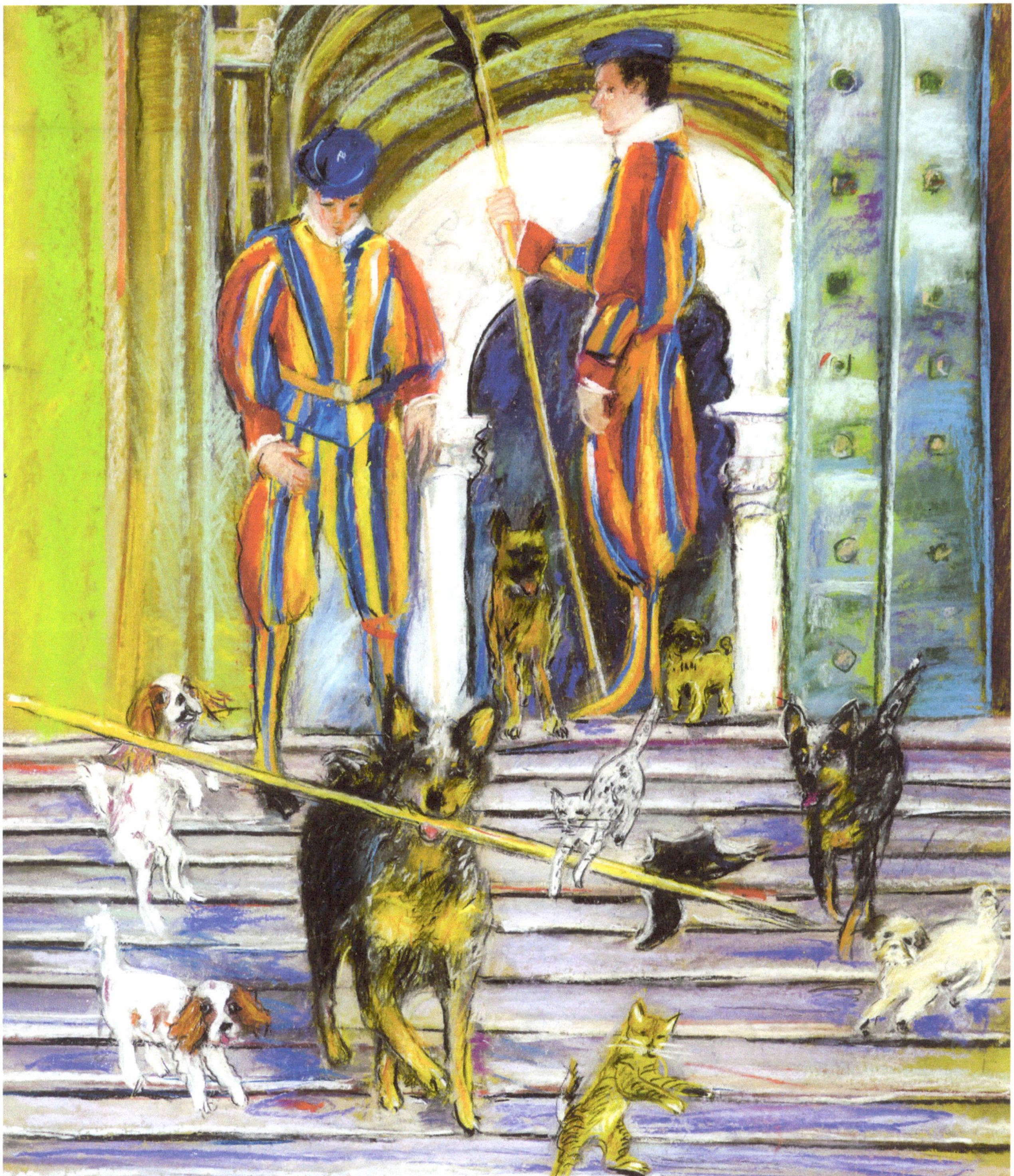

"Venice"

After arriving in Venice, Italy, the band of travelers go for a walk around St. Marks Square. Exhausted, they agree to take a leisurely tour on a gondola. Traveling in true Venetian style now.

With his newly acquired lance, Beaux is able to help the gondolier steer through all the canals. It's a "Grand" time.

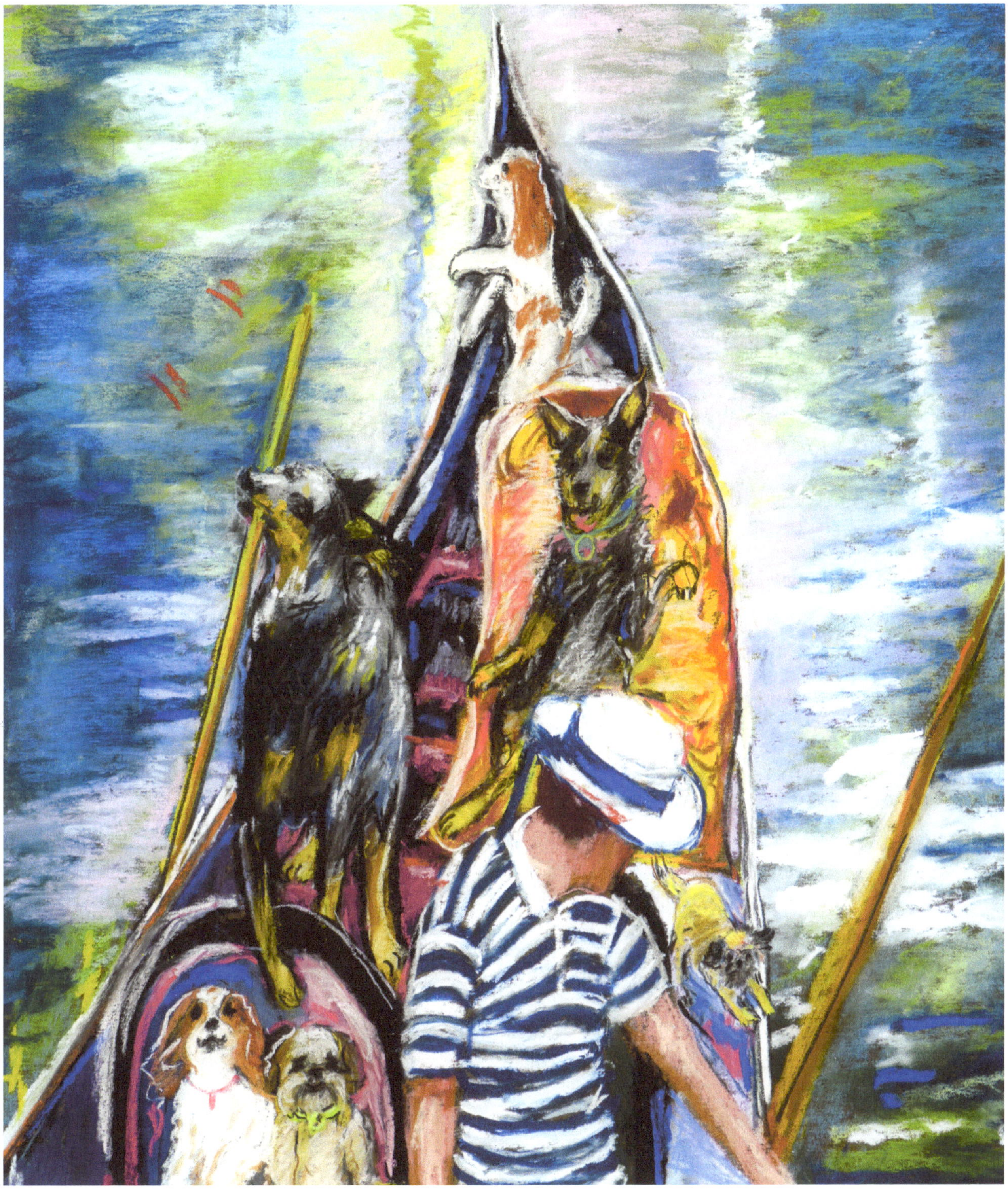

"I Can Dance Too"

While traveling through Vienna, Austria, the tour was able to visit the famous Lipizzan stallions. Watching them train in the stables, Beaux thought, "I can do that."

At the Performance Hall, Beaux is invited to dance at one of their sessions. His group is ecstatic when the audience cheers him on.

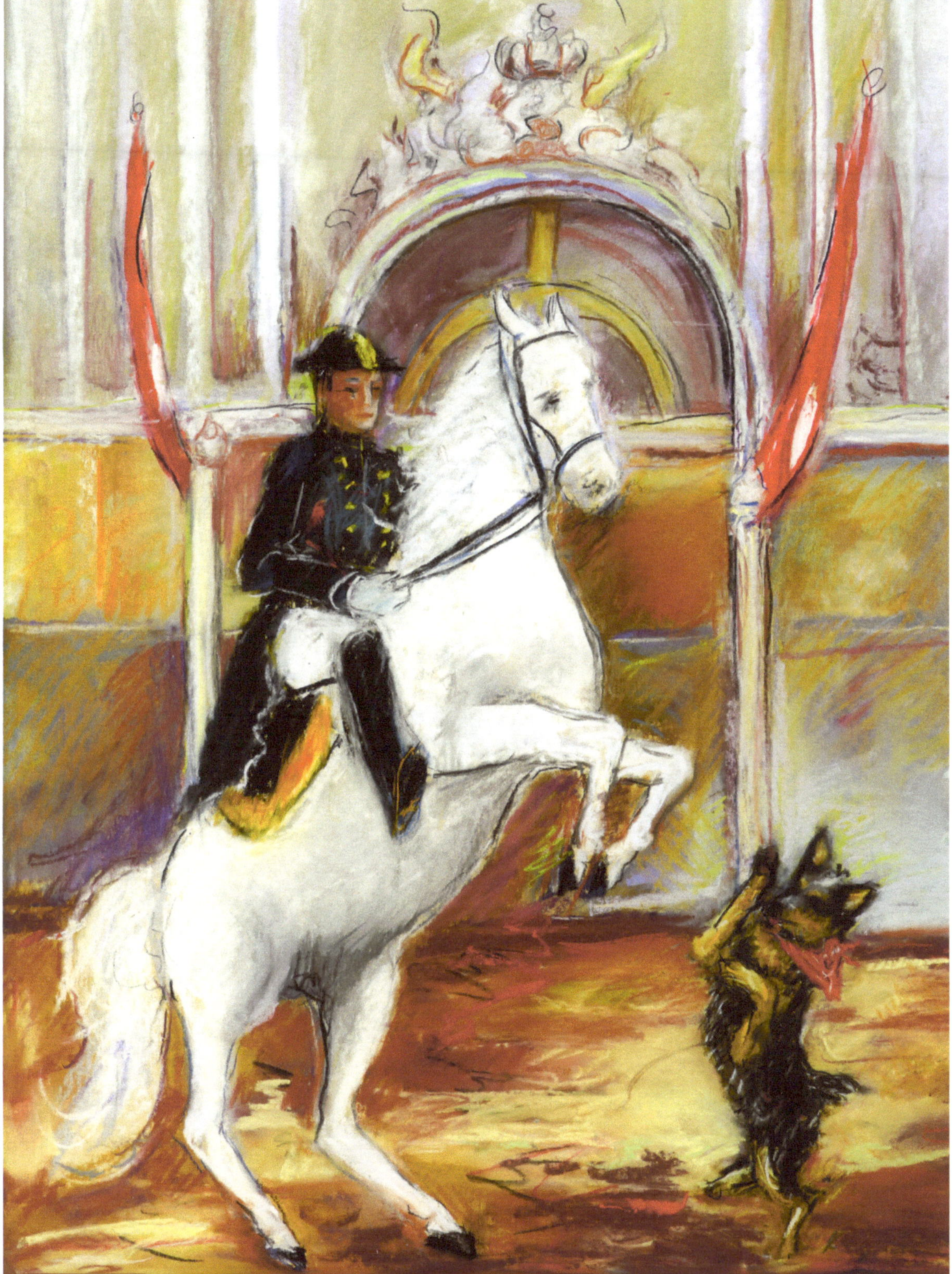

"Orient Express"

(Vienna to Paris)

A dream come true: "To Paris by train." Steven the Pullman oversees all the animals piling into one of the coaches. Jane B. Bailey and Lilly arrive late after one of their frequent shopping sprees. "Now on to our fantasy trip," Beaux and his menagerie could hardly contain themselves.

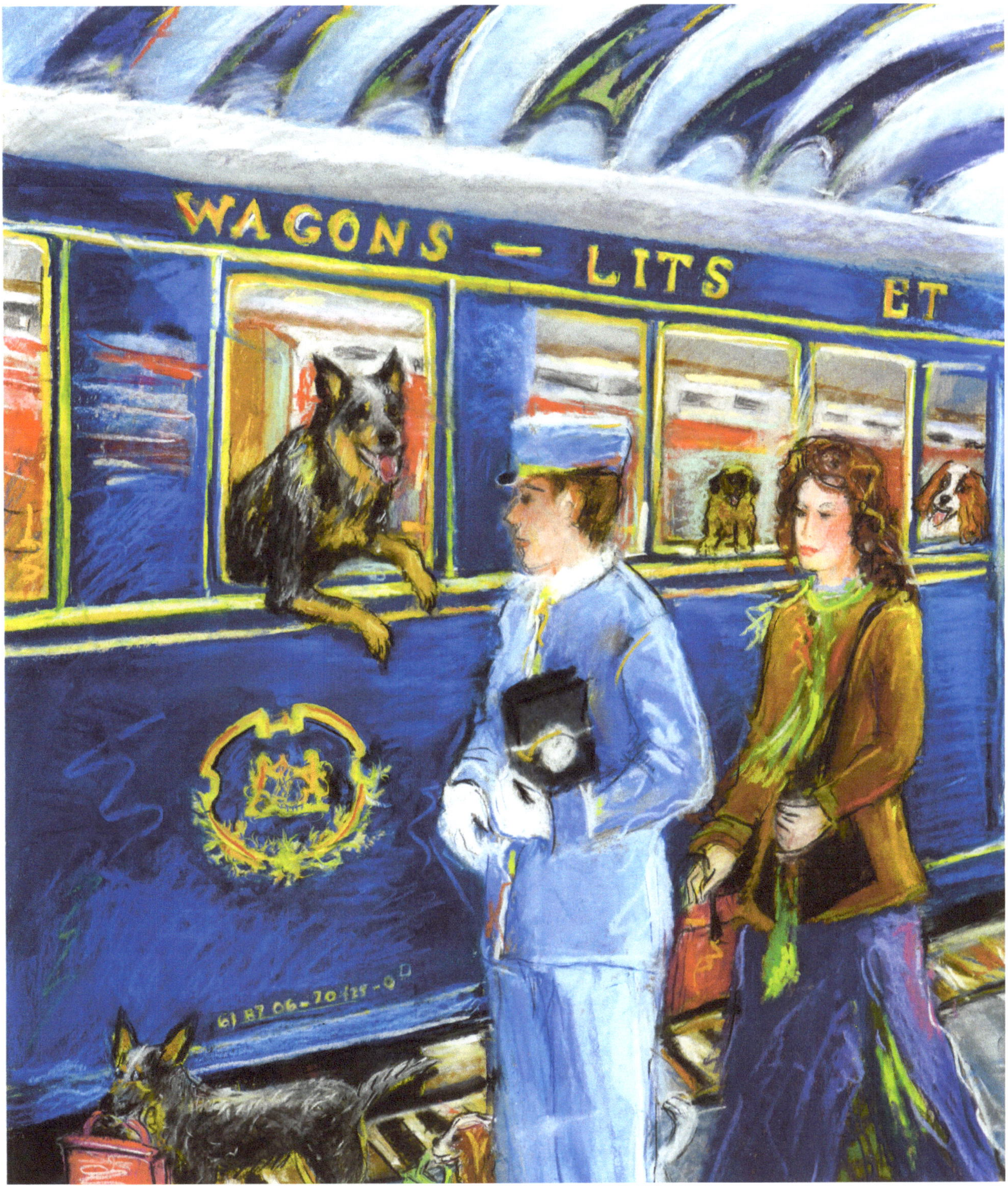
WAGONS — LITS
ET

"Back to Paris"

It's a great day to play in the shadow of the Eiffel Tower. The cats love chasing the butterflies. Mina, the German shepherd, enjoys playing with the cats. Bertie chases his friend the squirrel to exhaustion. Beaux and Bailey are now a pair. A photographer comes along and asks if he can take their picture. "Sure, why not?"

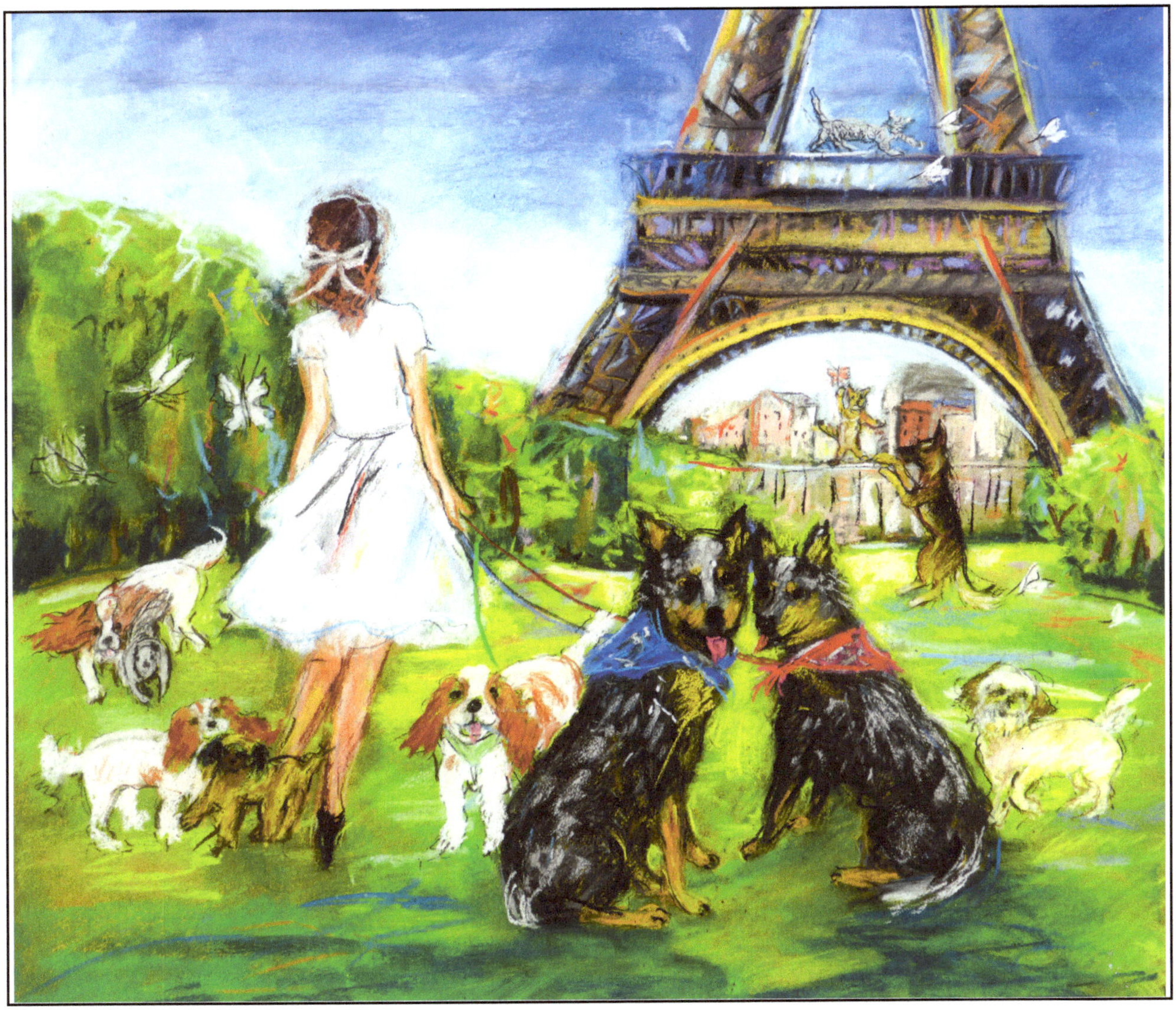

"Monet Gardens"

Bailey, Lilly, and Chou-Chou take a side trip into Monet's Garden. While on a boat near the famous Blue Green Bridge, they had an artistic inspiration. "Let's go on an open-air painting safari!" Bailey declared.

Bailey painted some lilies, Chou-Chou decided to work on the background colors, while Lilly does the boat and the human. Quite an accomplishment, don't you think?

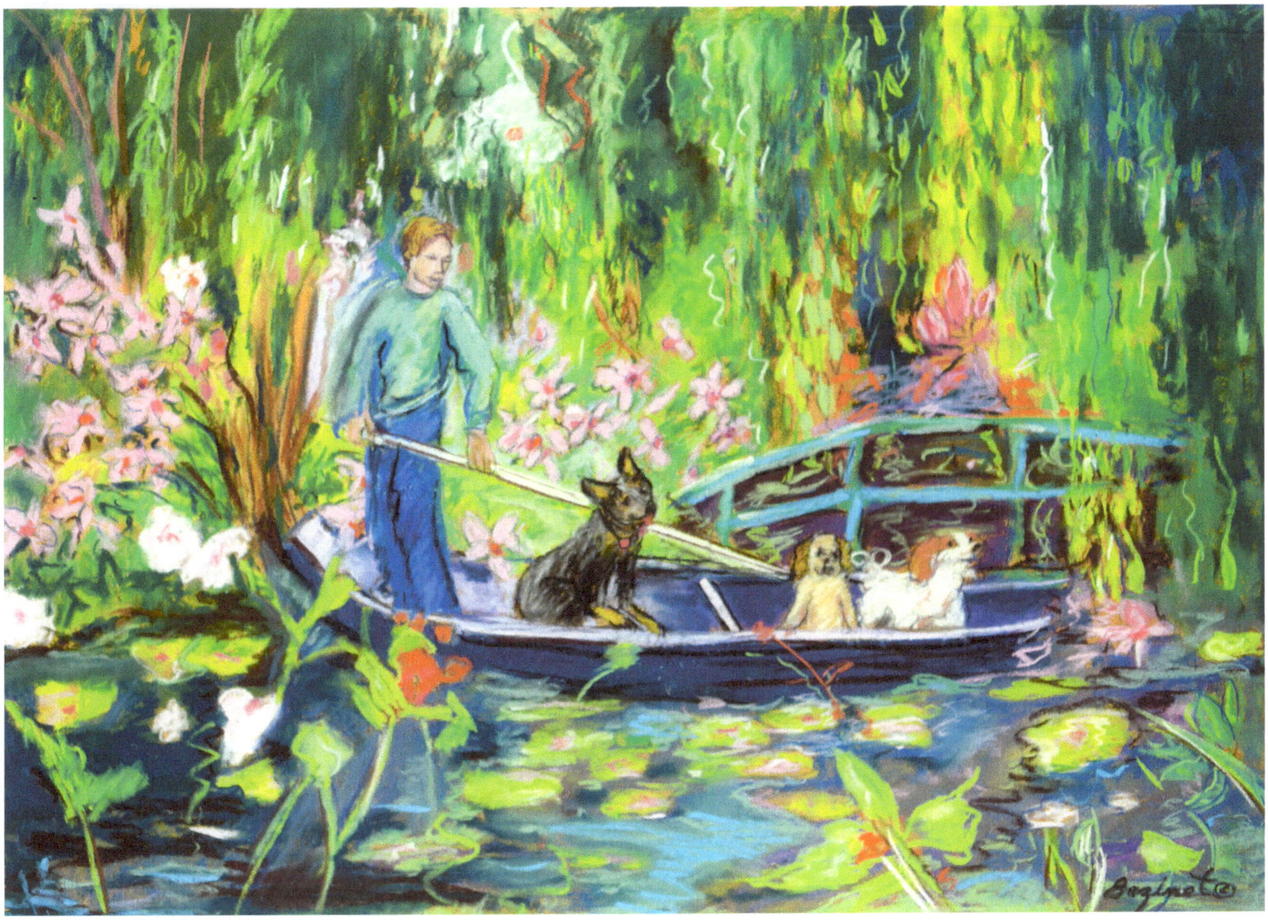

“Beaux's Tour Bus”

Arriving in London, Beaux is compelled to purchase a tour bus to accommodate his many followers. They have come to see Harry Potter and tour the Tower, the Eye, London Bridge, and—not to forget—Putney. (Jane B.'s former residence).

They crowded into a phone booth for fun, rented scooters and ran around the Underground platform. Great times!

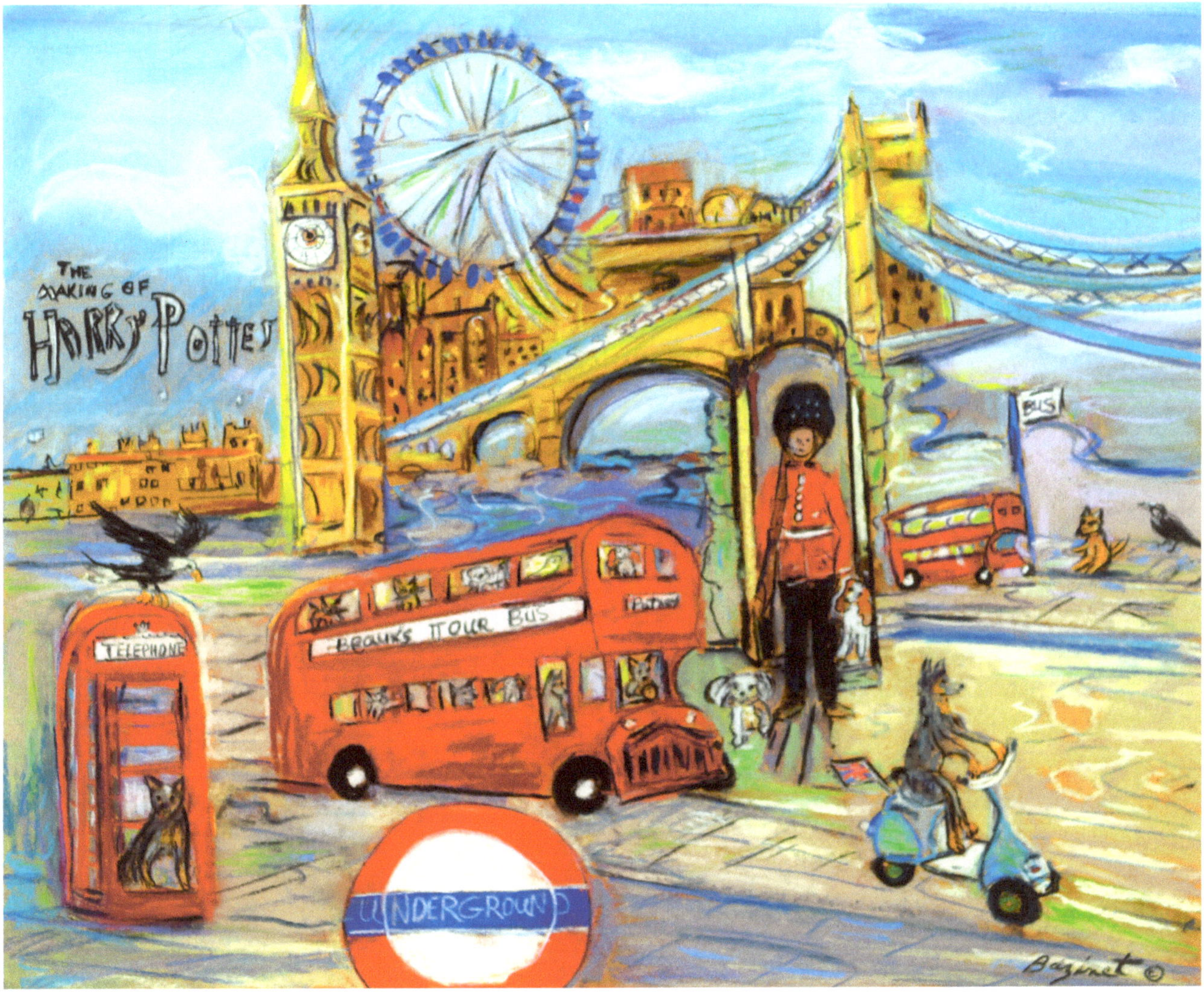
THE MAKING OF
HARRY POTTER
TELEPHONE
BROWN'S TOUR BUS
BUS
UNDERGROUND
Bazinet ©

"Hyde Park"

Hyde Park, one of the largest parks in London, is split in two by a river called the Serpentine. It's a wonderful place to meet black swans, Egyptian geese, and minibeast.

Playing with balls, throwing frisbees, and chasing butterflies was the highlight of a leisurely day.

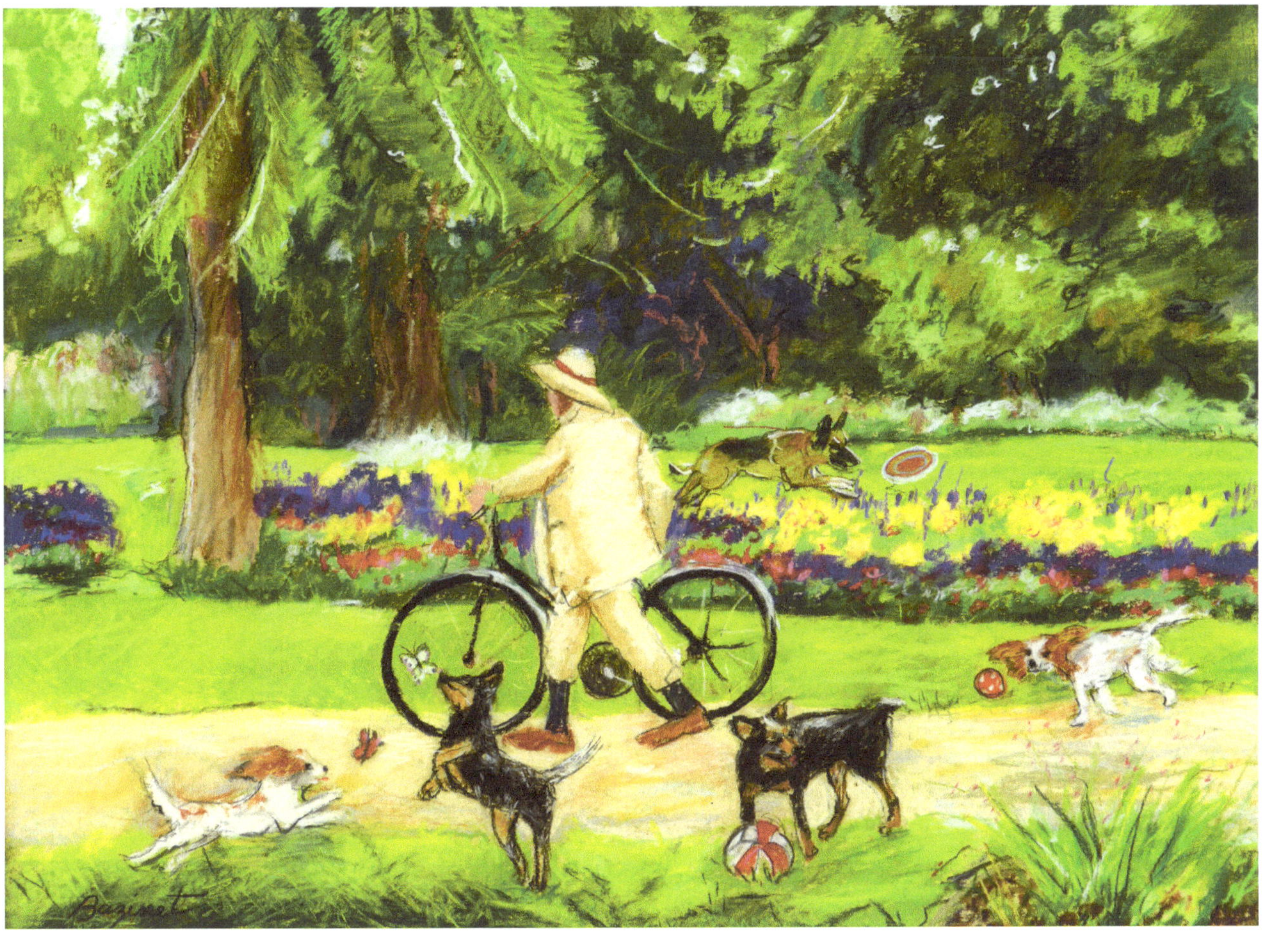

"The Tate Gallery"

Ms. Macdonald takes some of the girls to the Tate in London. They all want to know, what is a "Picasso?" They learned he was one of the founders of the Cubist style of painting. They were surprised he also was a sculptor, printmaker, ceramicist, poet, and a playwright!

At the end of their visit, they just must have Afternoon Tea.

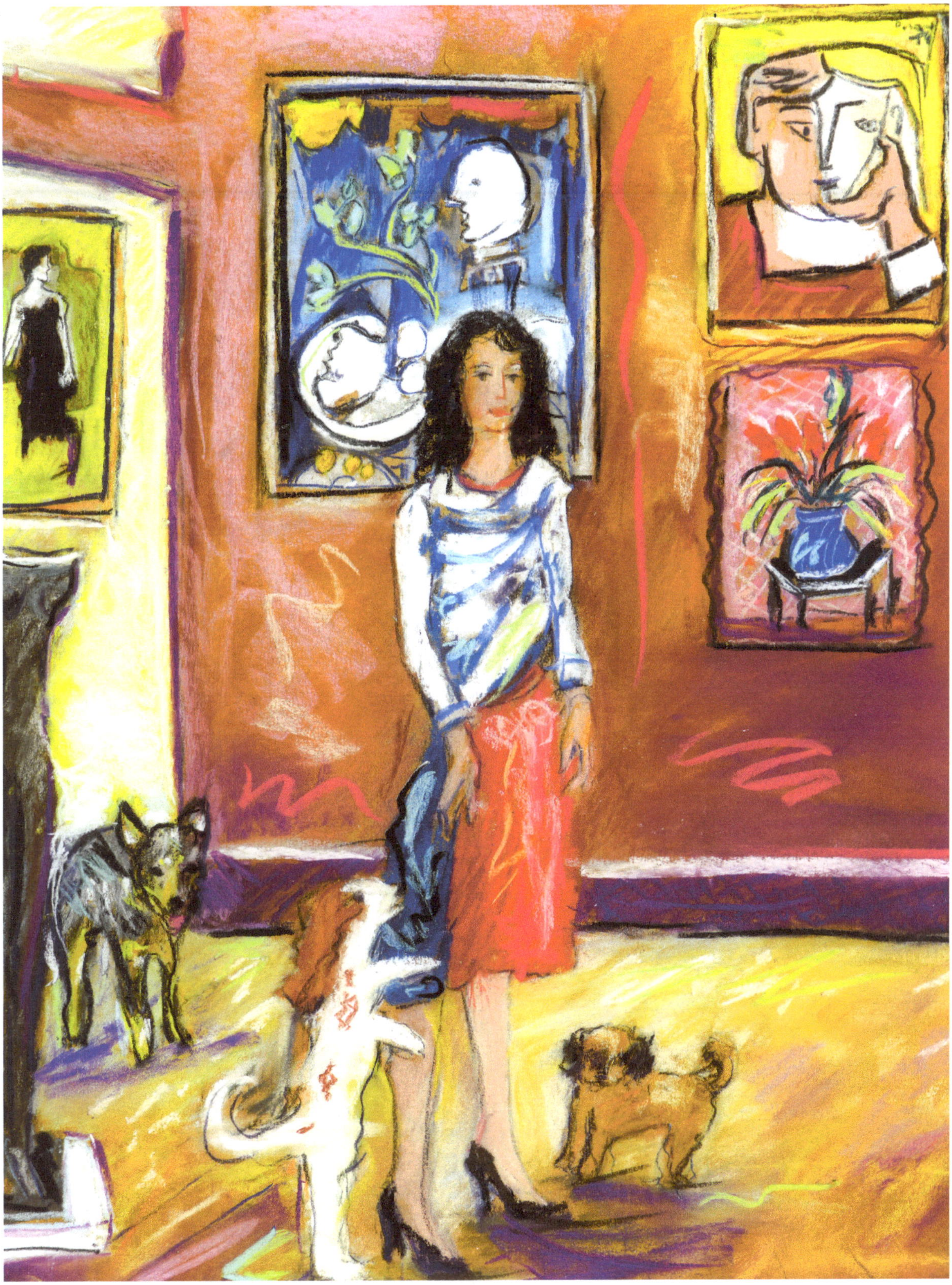

"Poochi Biking"

At the end of the tour, Beaux and Jane B. bid Au Revoir to all of their faithful clients. They decide to take a short trip to Ashford Castle in Ireland for some cycling and much needed rest.

The tour was a great success and word has spread. Beaux's next excursion is already booked!

With a look to the future, he decides it's time to invest in a plane. WOW!

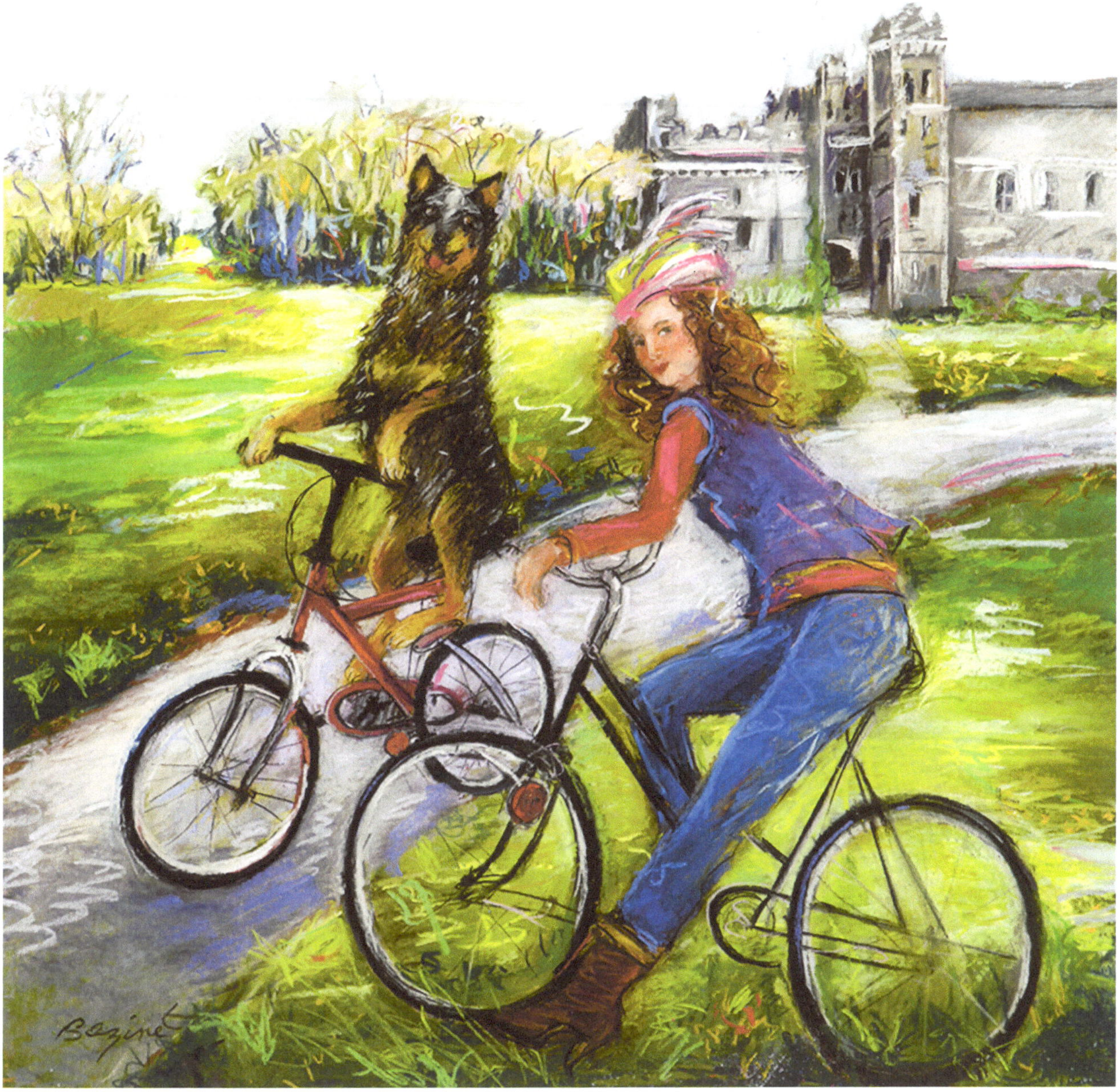
Bezinet

"Australian Cattle Dog Airline"

Owned and operated by Blue Heelers

(Beaux and friends next adventure - North America)

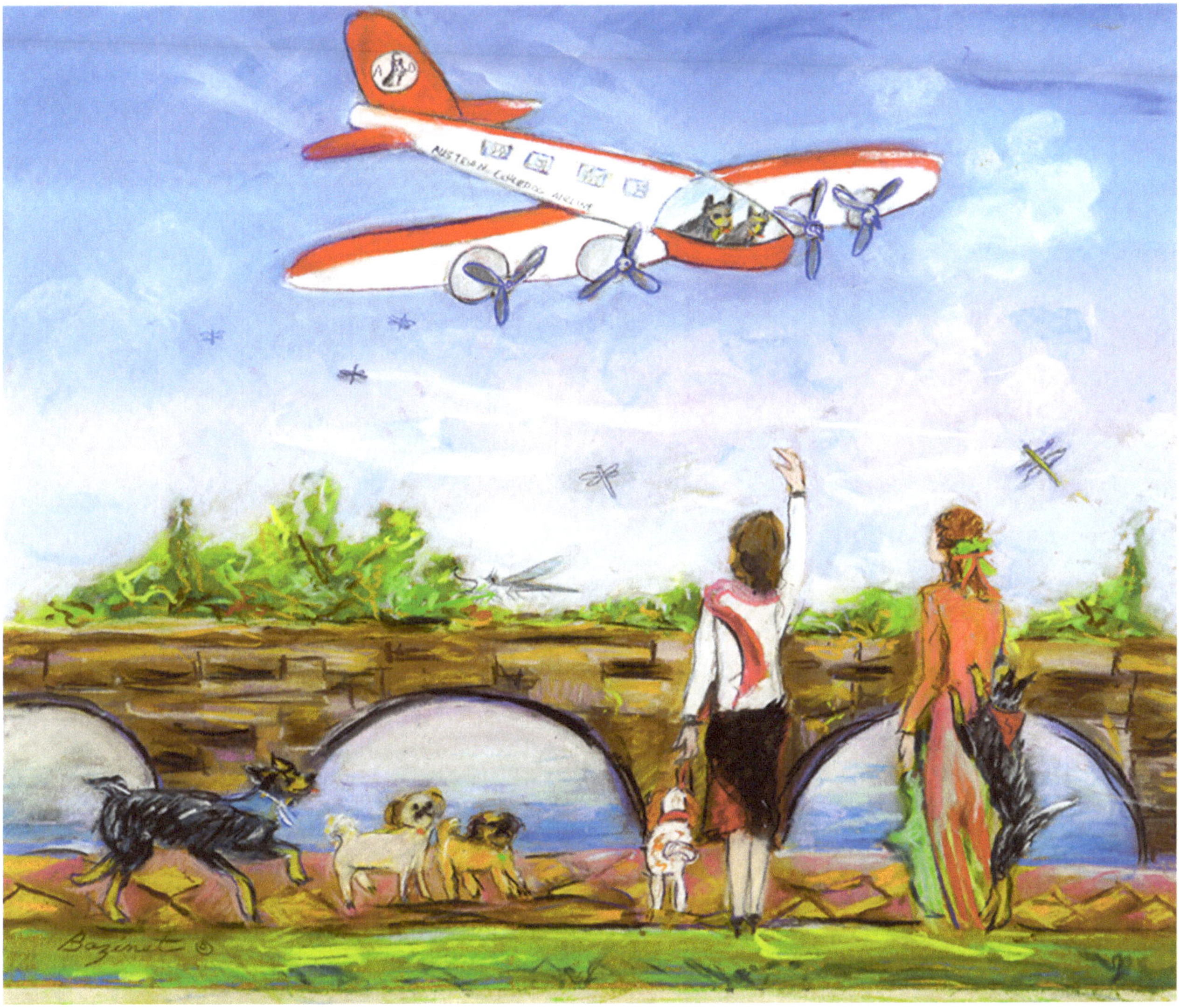
Bazinet ©

Coloring Pages

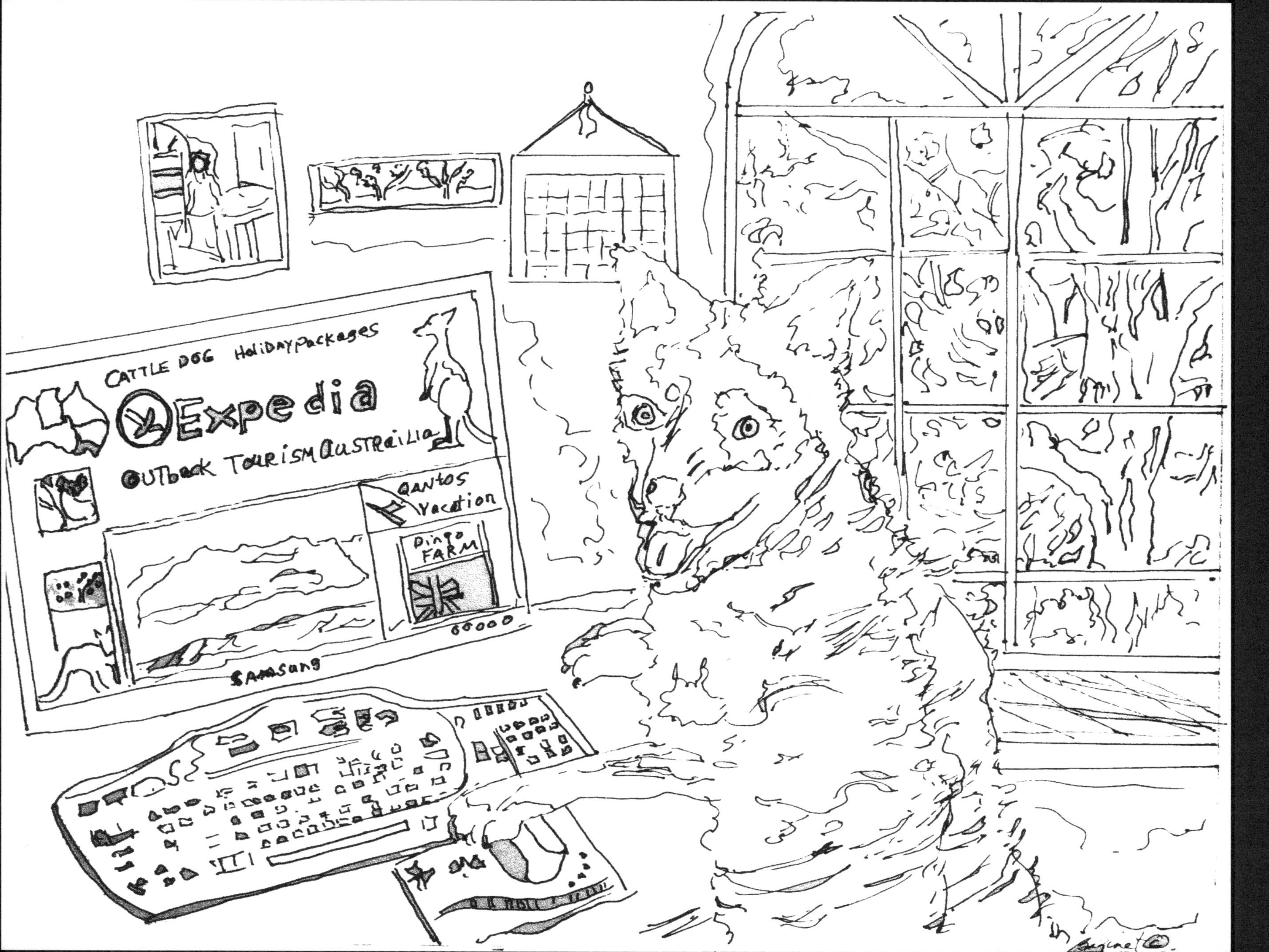
CATTLE DOG HolidayPackages
Expedia
OUTback TOURISM AUSTRAILIA
Qantos Vacation
Dingo FARM
$0000
SAMSUNG

"Cattle Dog Holiday Packages"

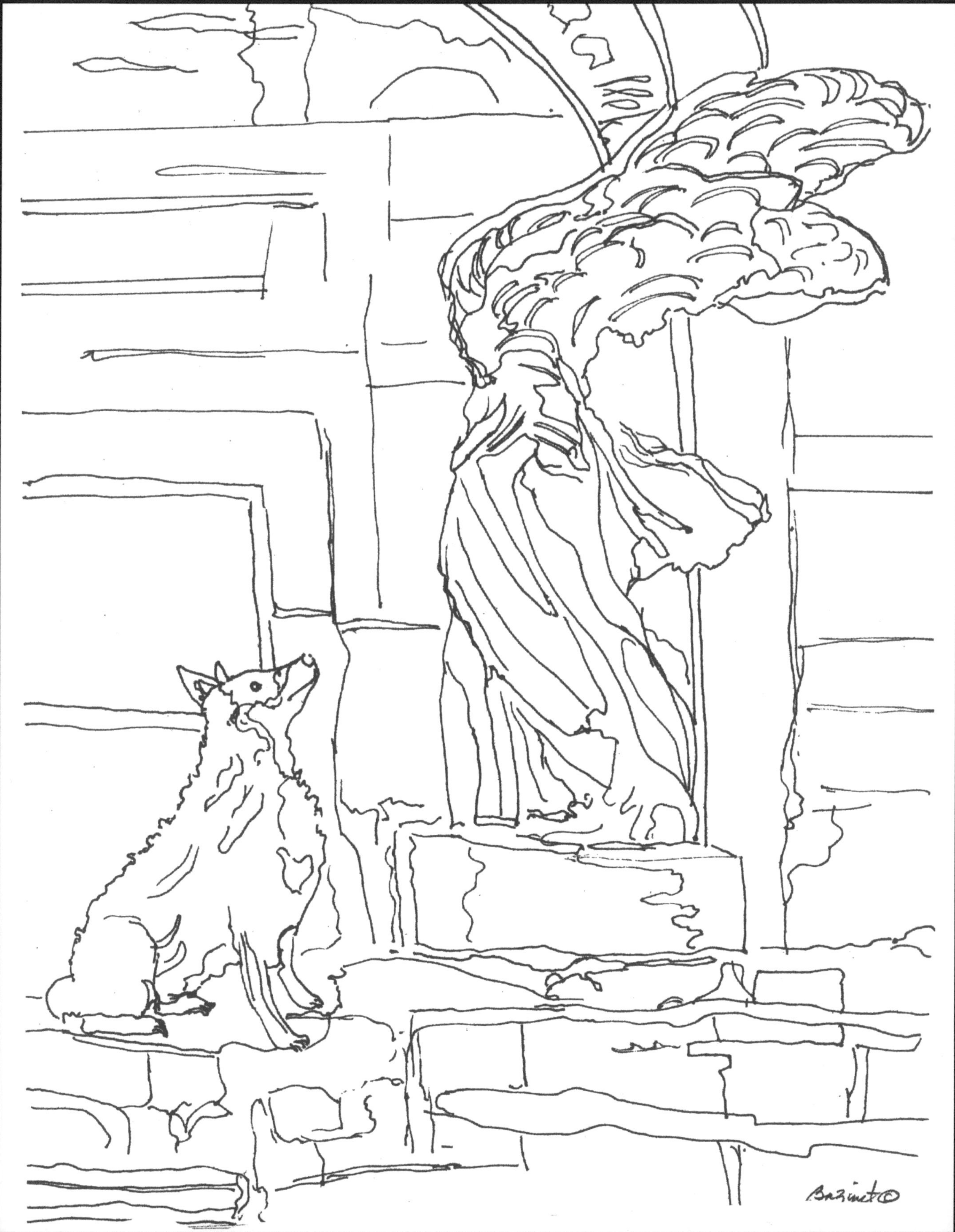
Bazinet©

"Where's Her Head?"

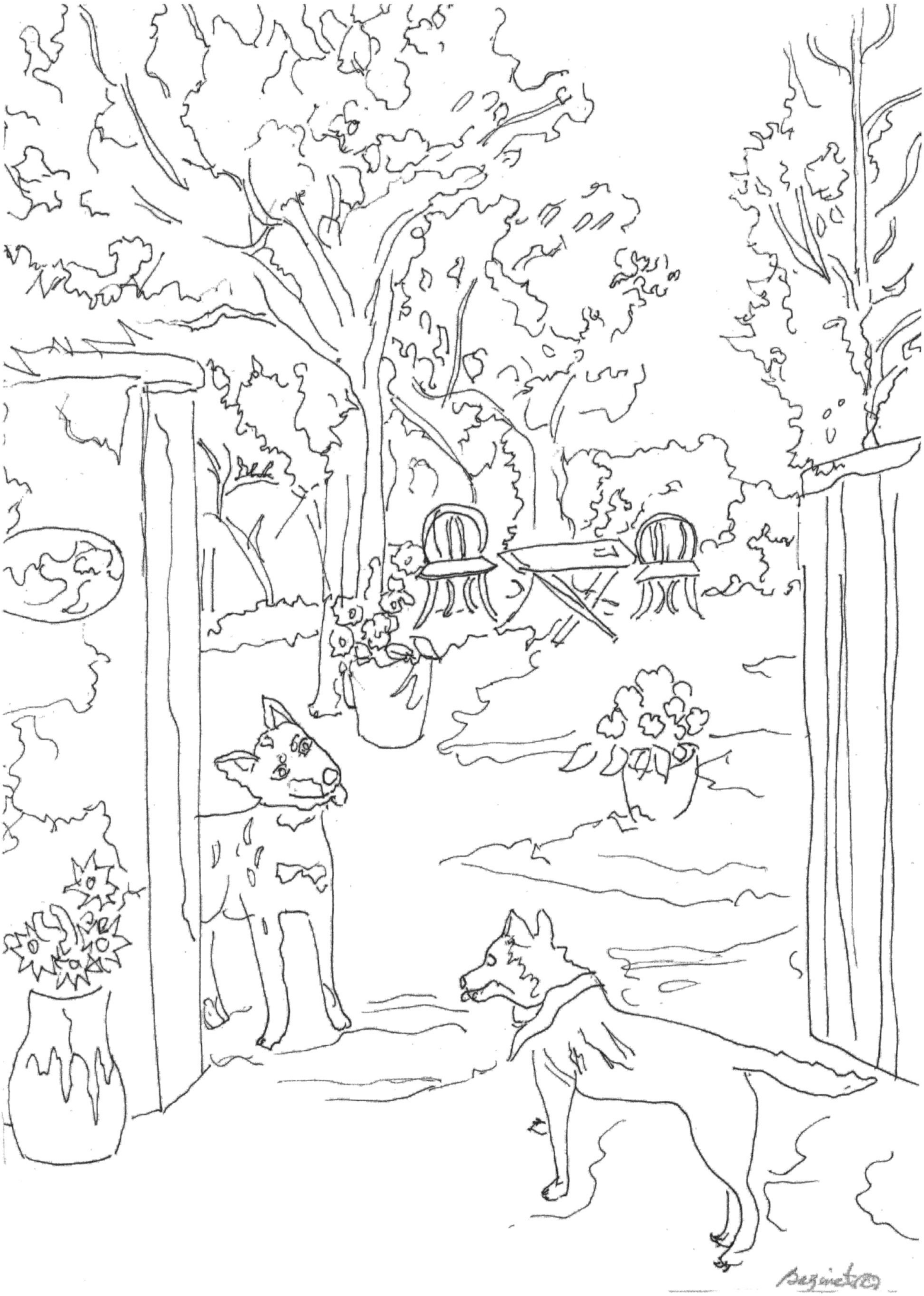

"Châteaurenard"

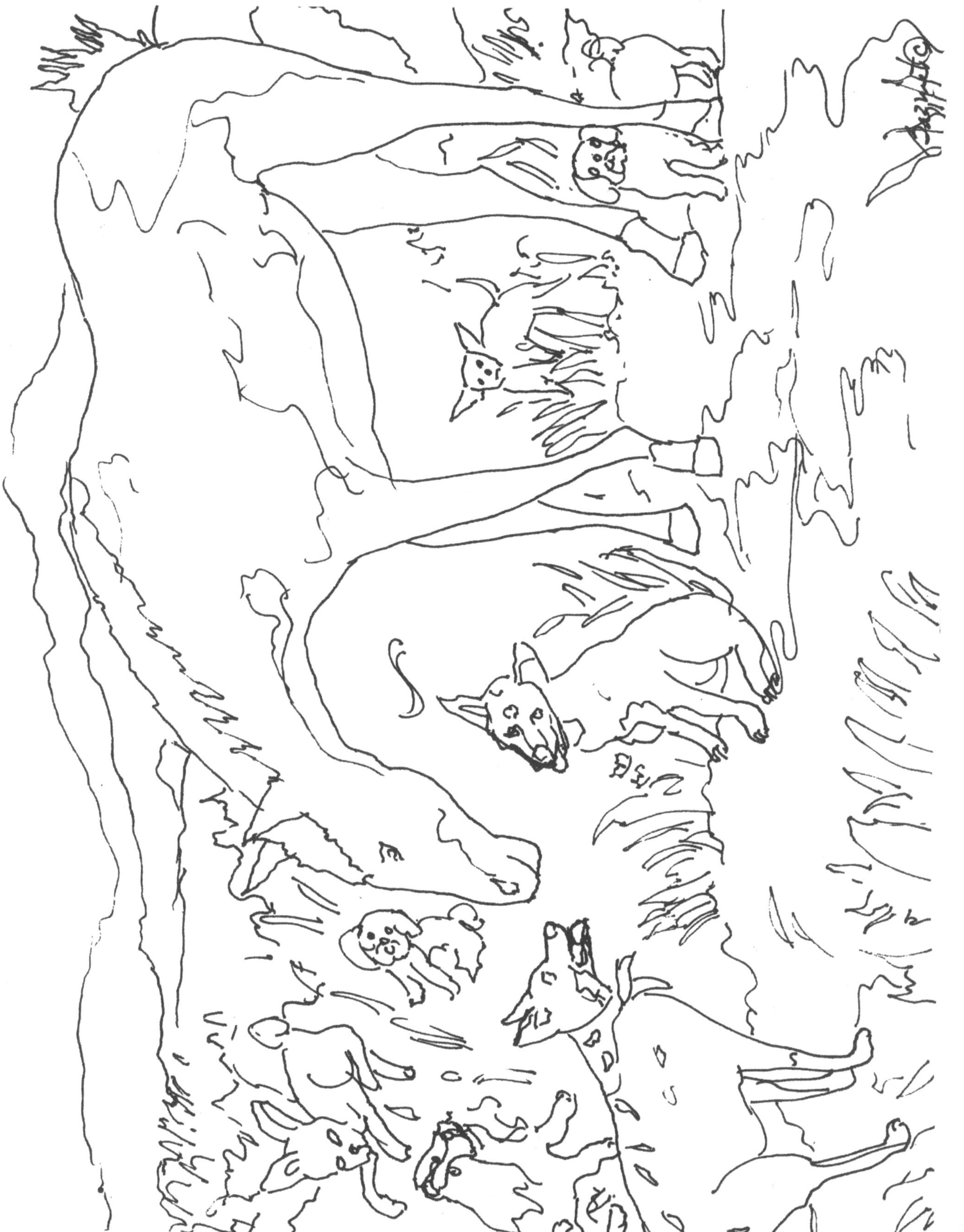

“La Camarque”

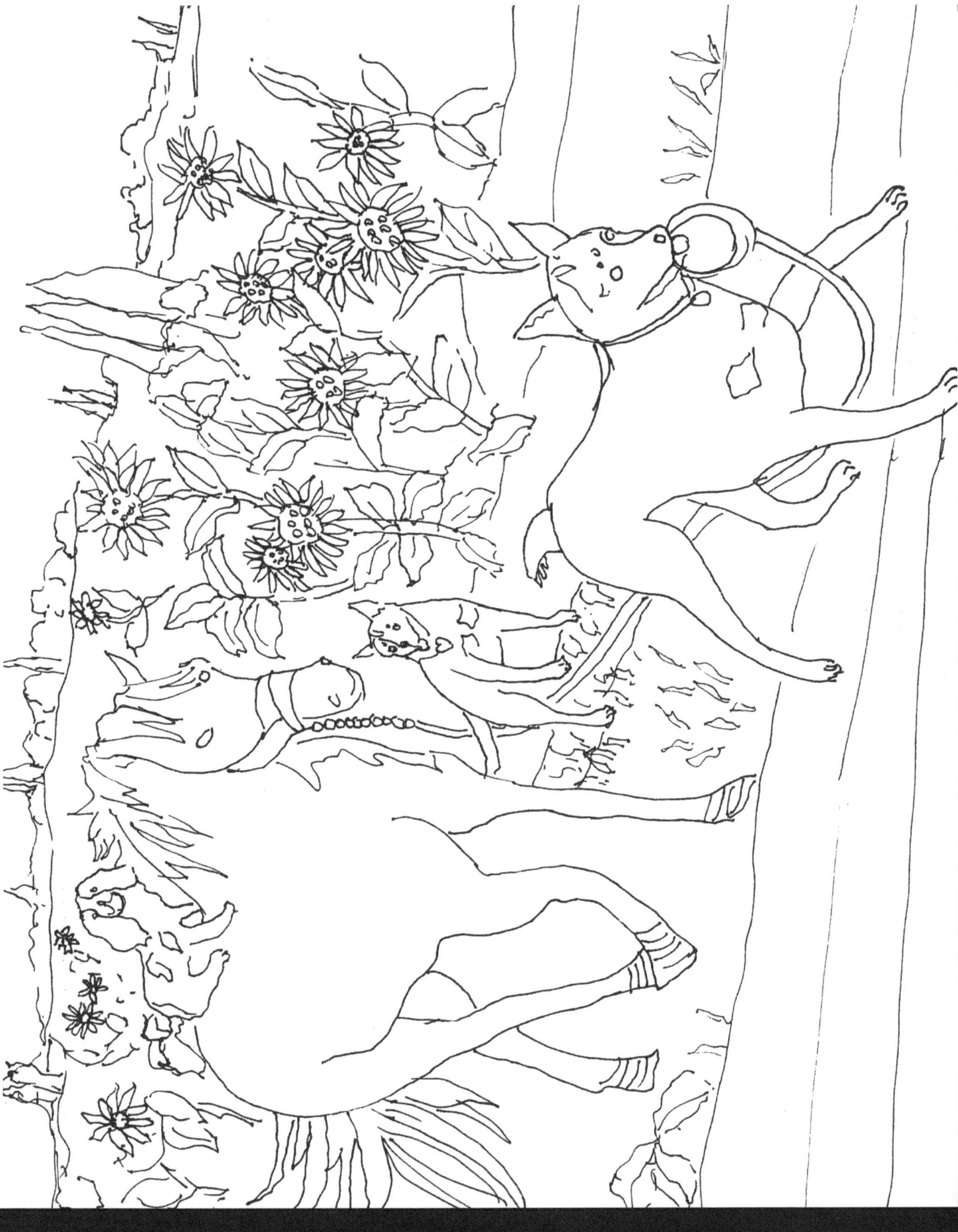

"Sunflower Fields"

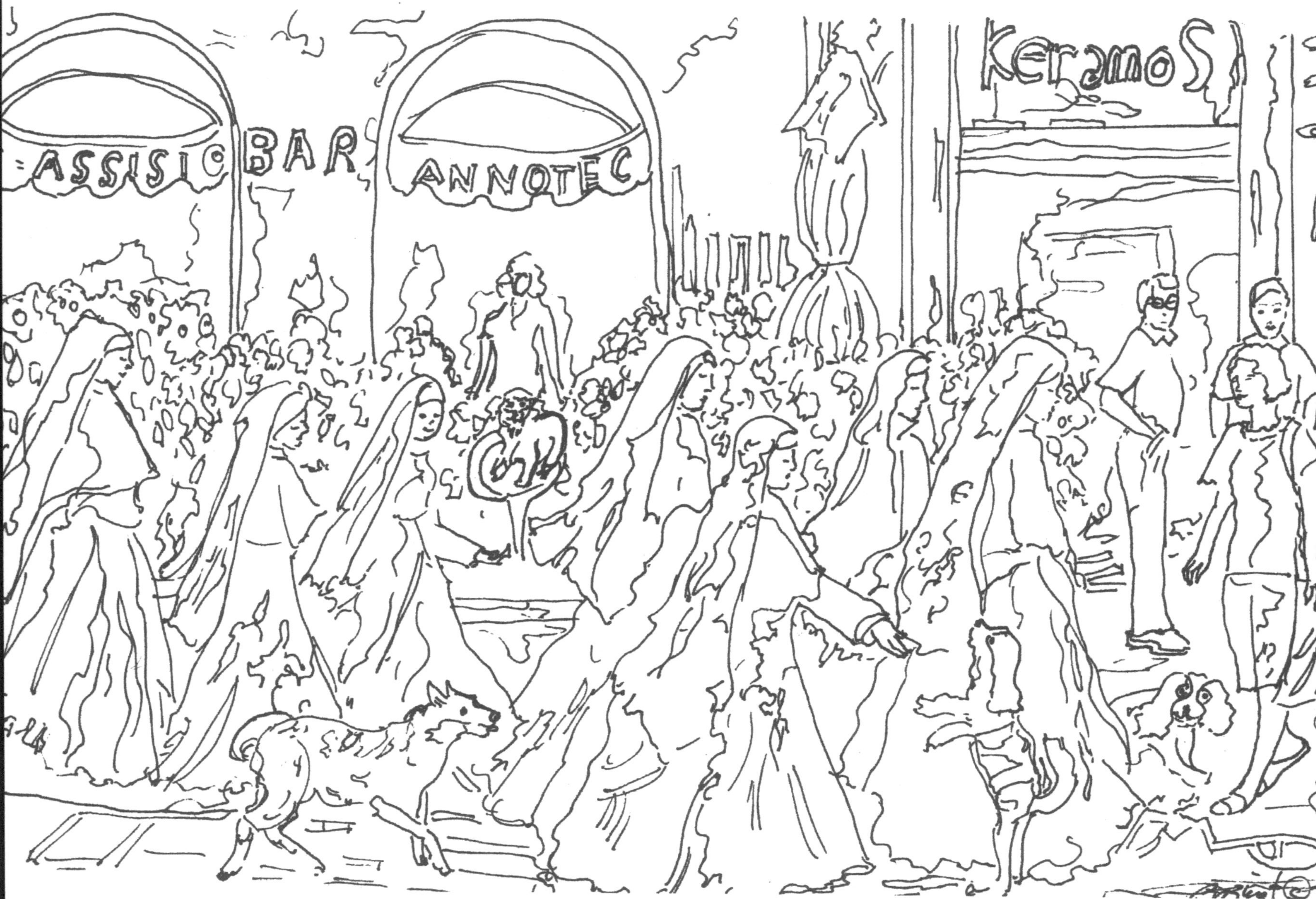
ASSISI
BAR
ANNOTEC
KeramoS

"Asissi"

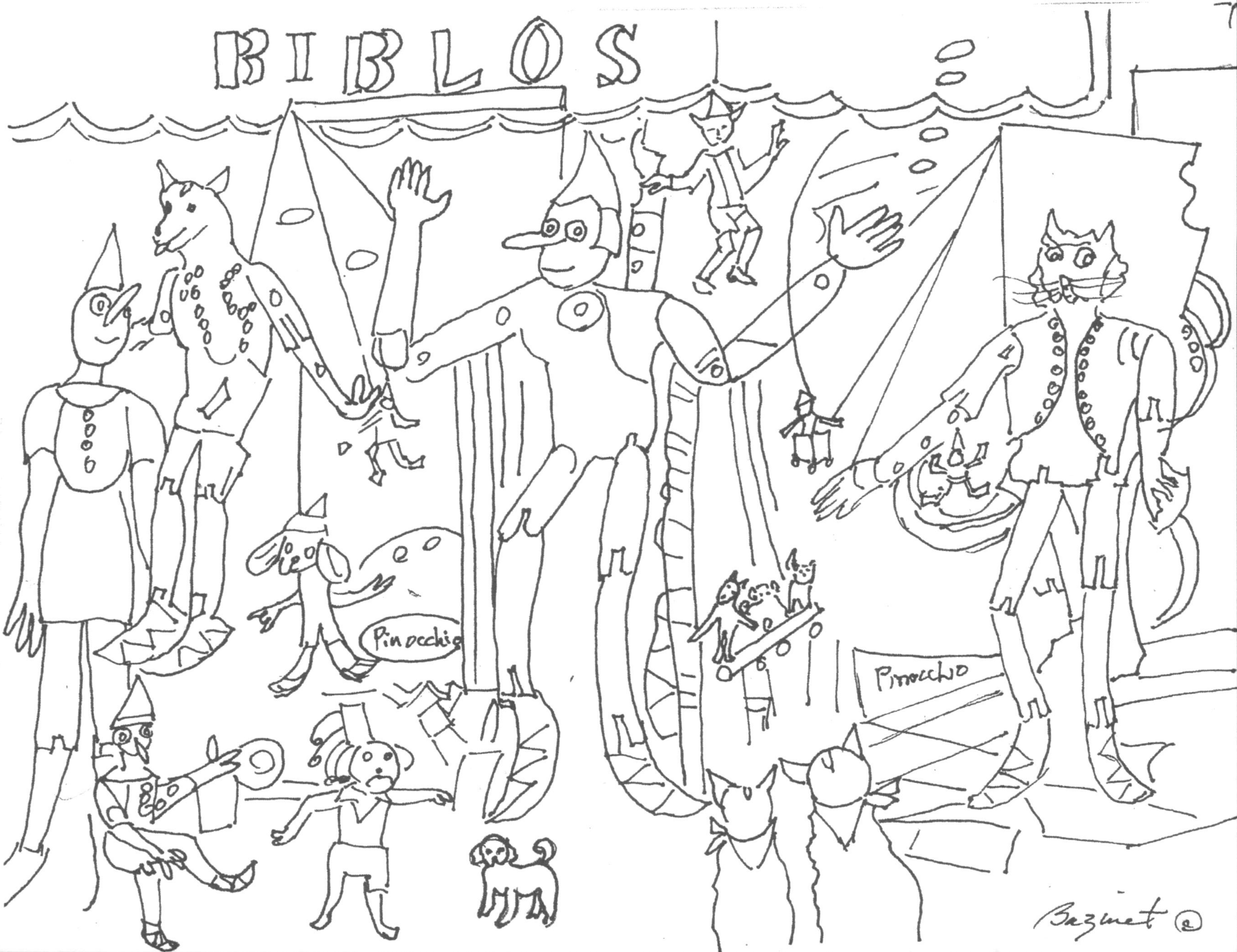
BIBLOS
Pinocchio
Pinocchio
Bazinet ©

"Biblos"

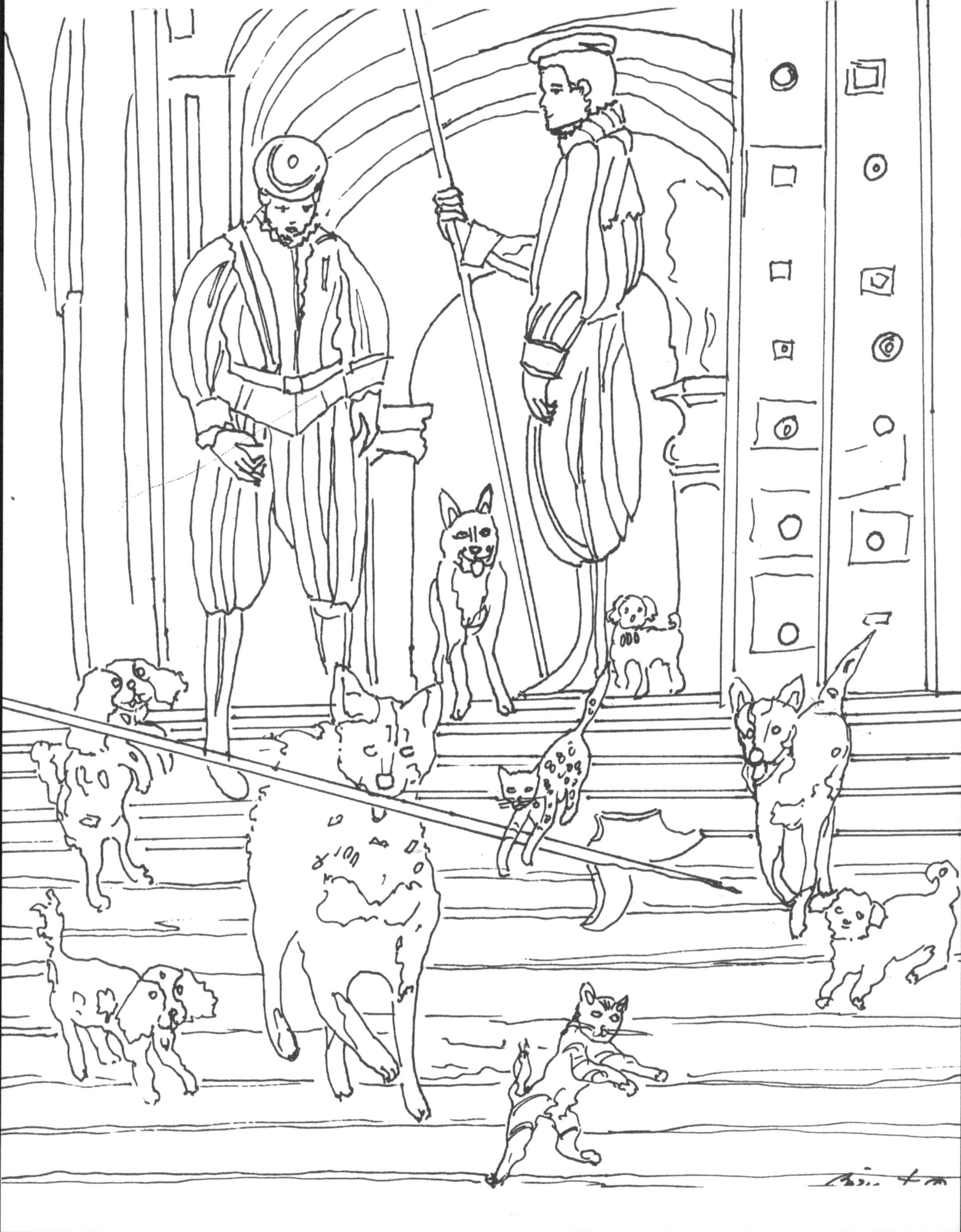

"The Vatican"

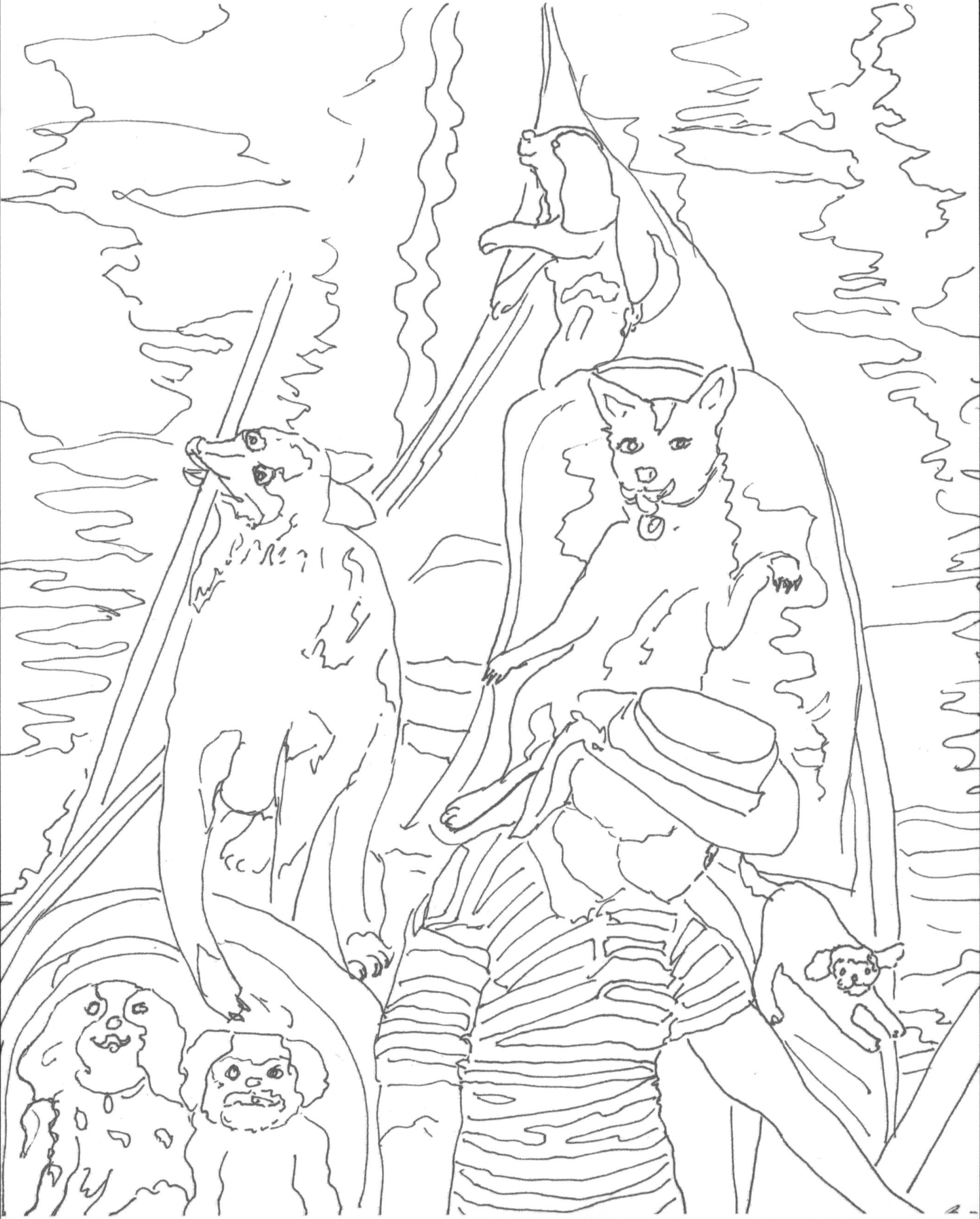

“Venice”

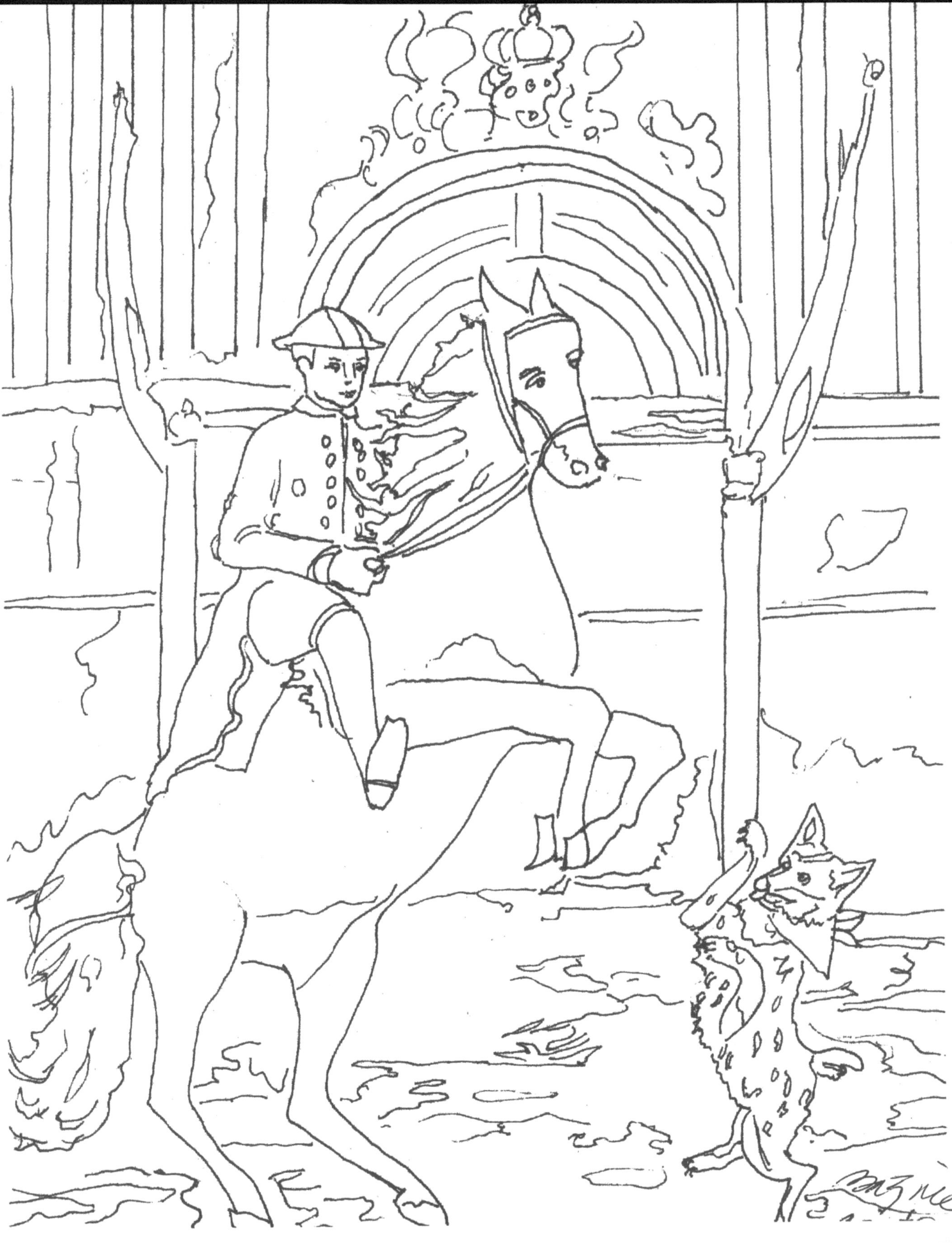

“I Can Dance Too”

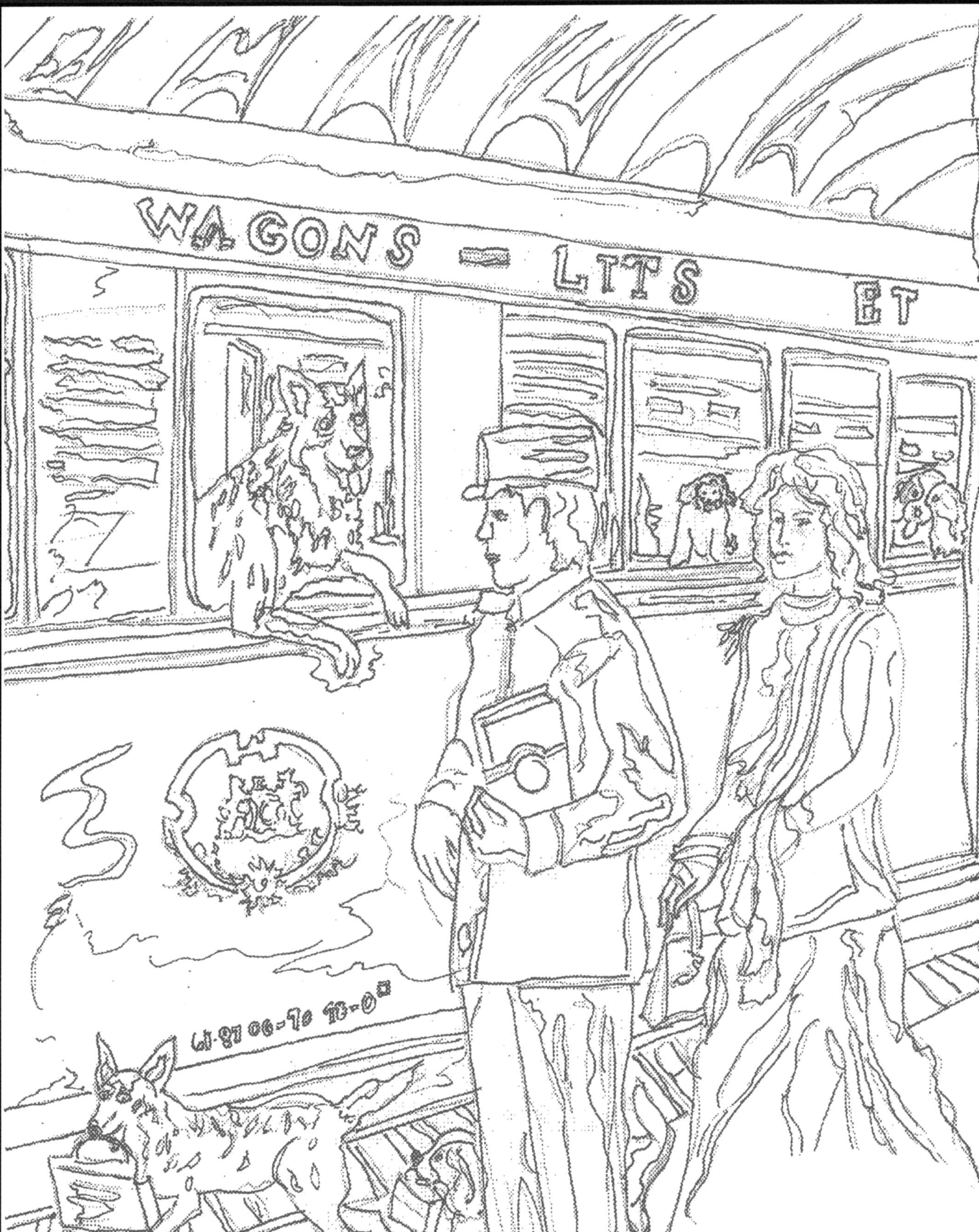
WAGONS — LITS
ET

“Orient Express”

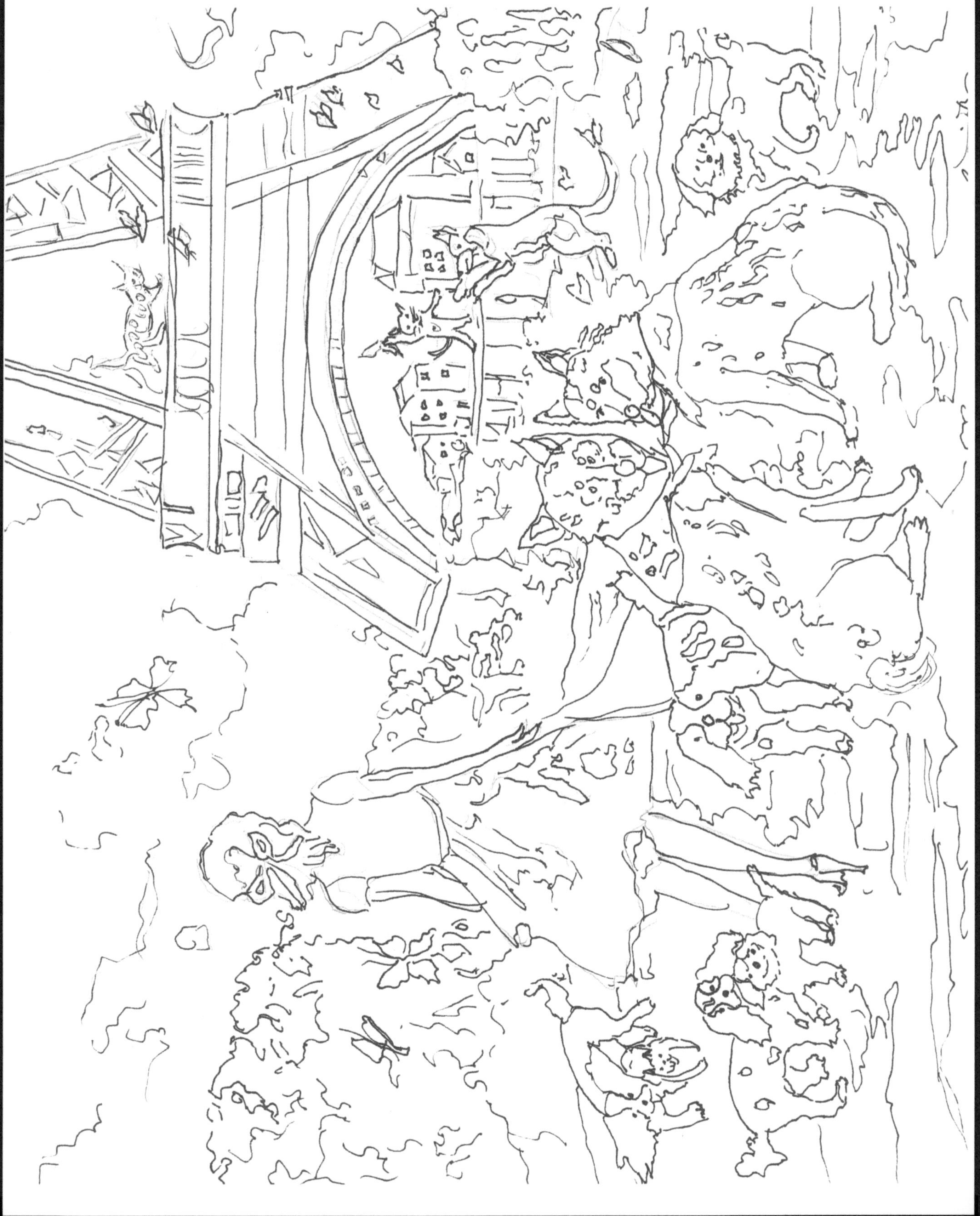

"Back to Paris"

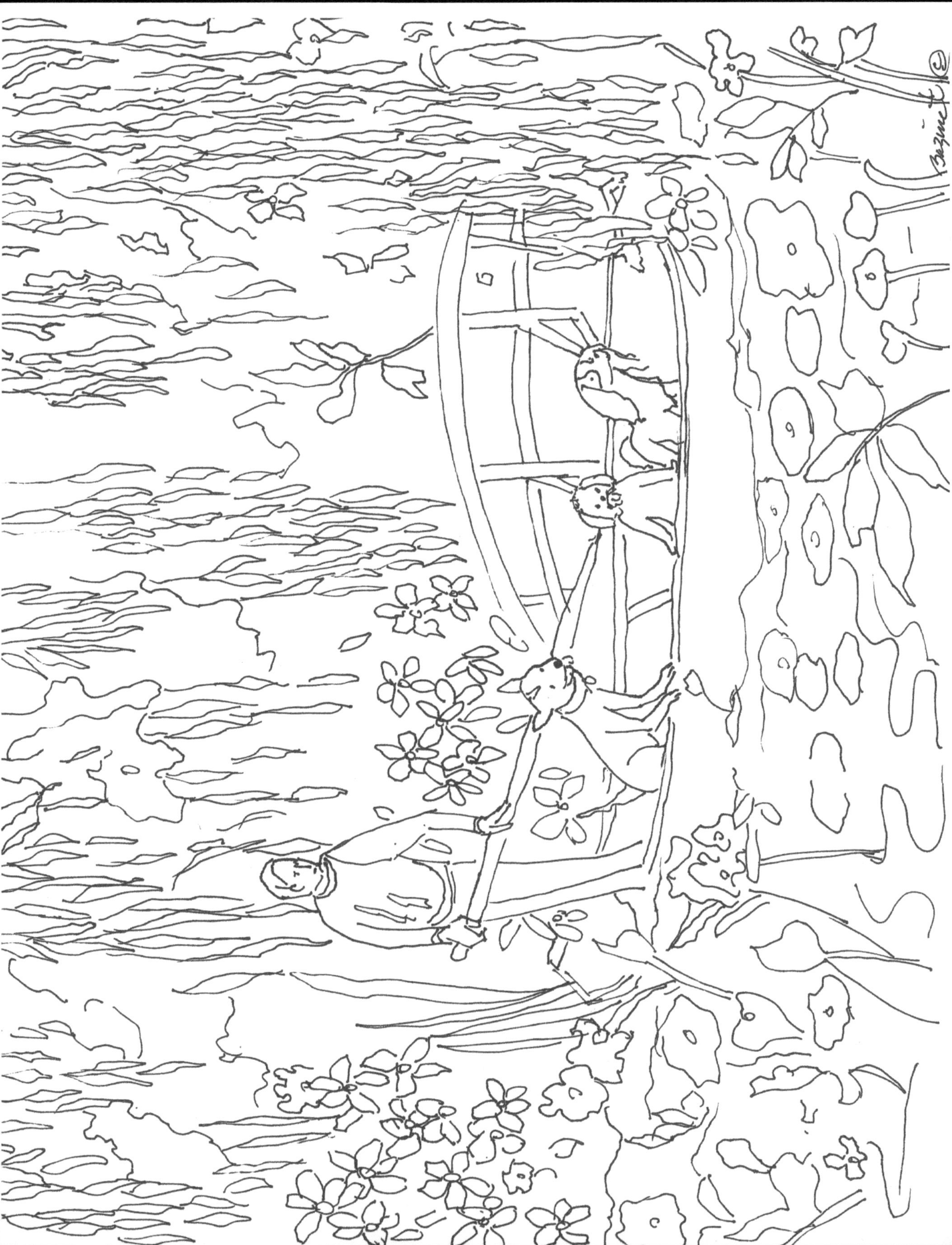

"Monet Gardens"

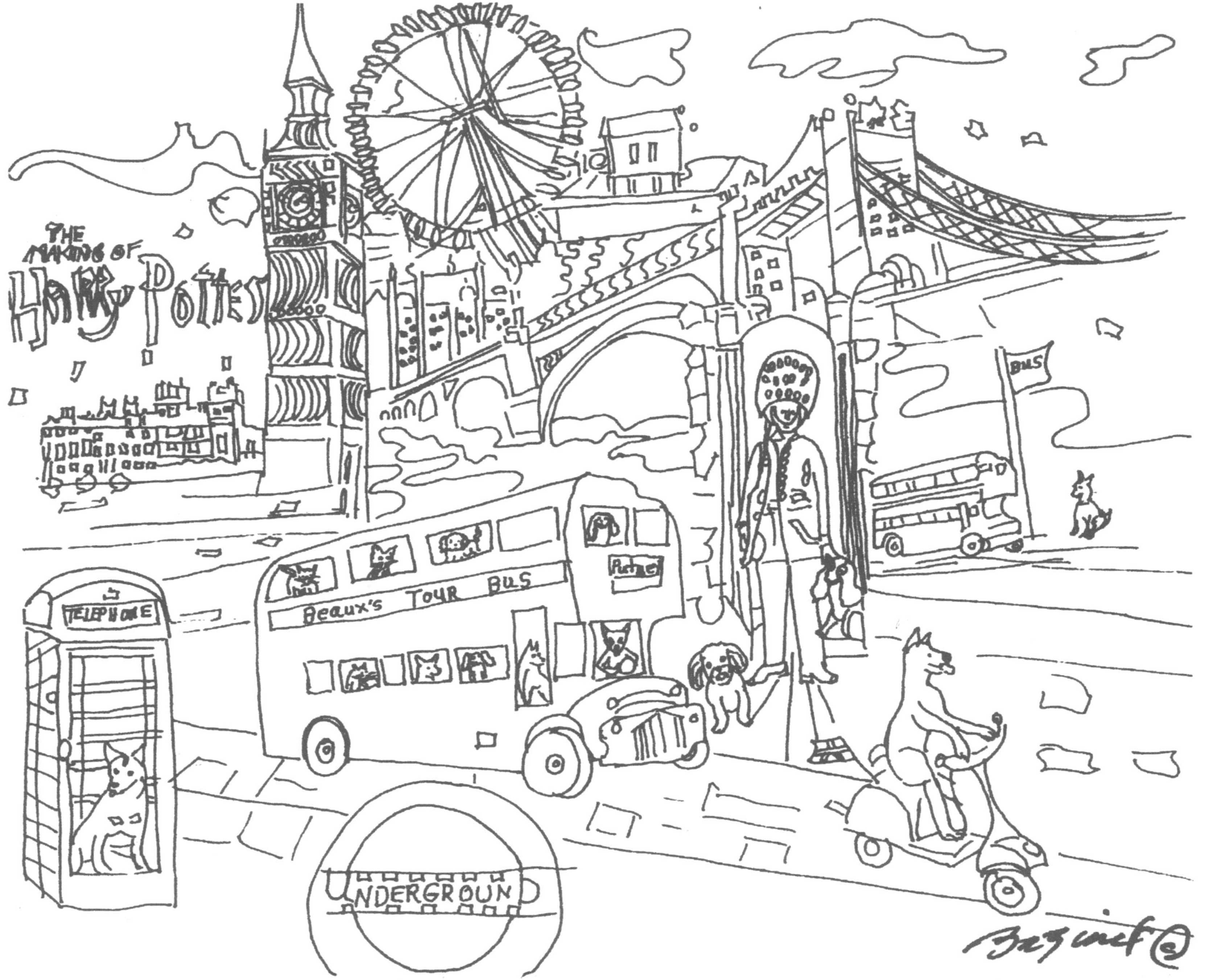
THE MAKING OF Harry Potter
BUS
Beaux's TOUR BUS
TELEPHONE
UNDERGROUND

"Beaux's Tour Bus"

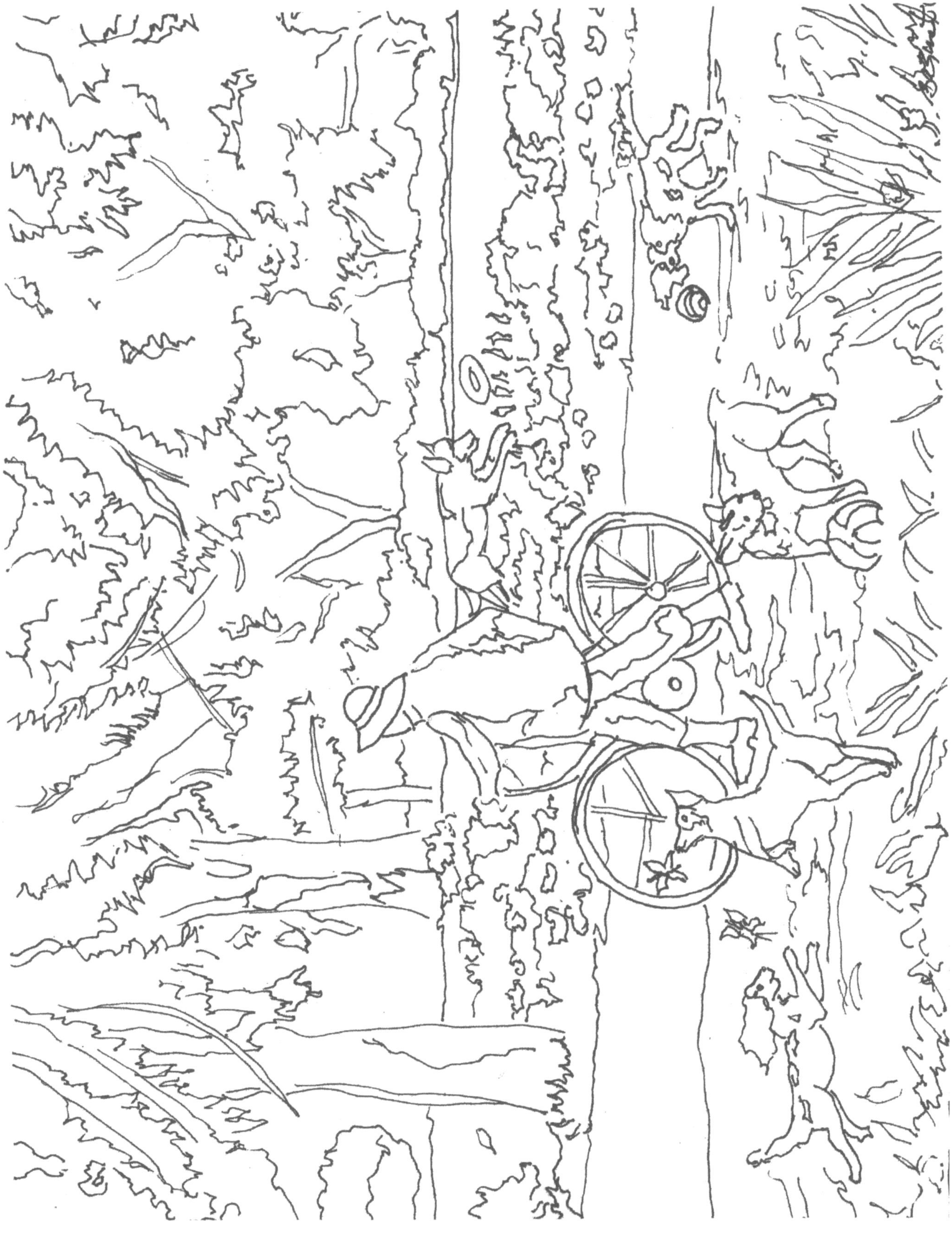

"Hyde Park"

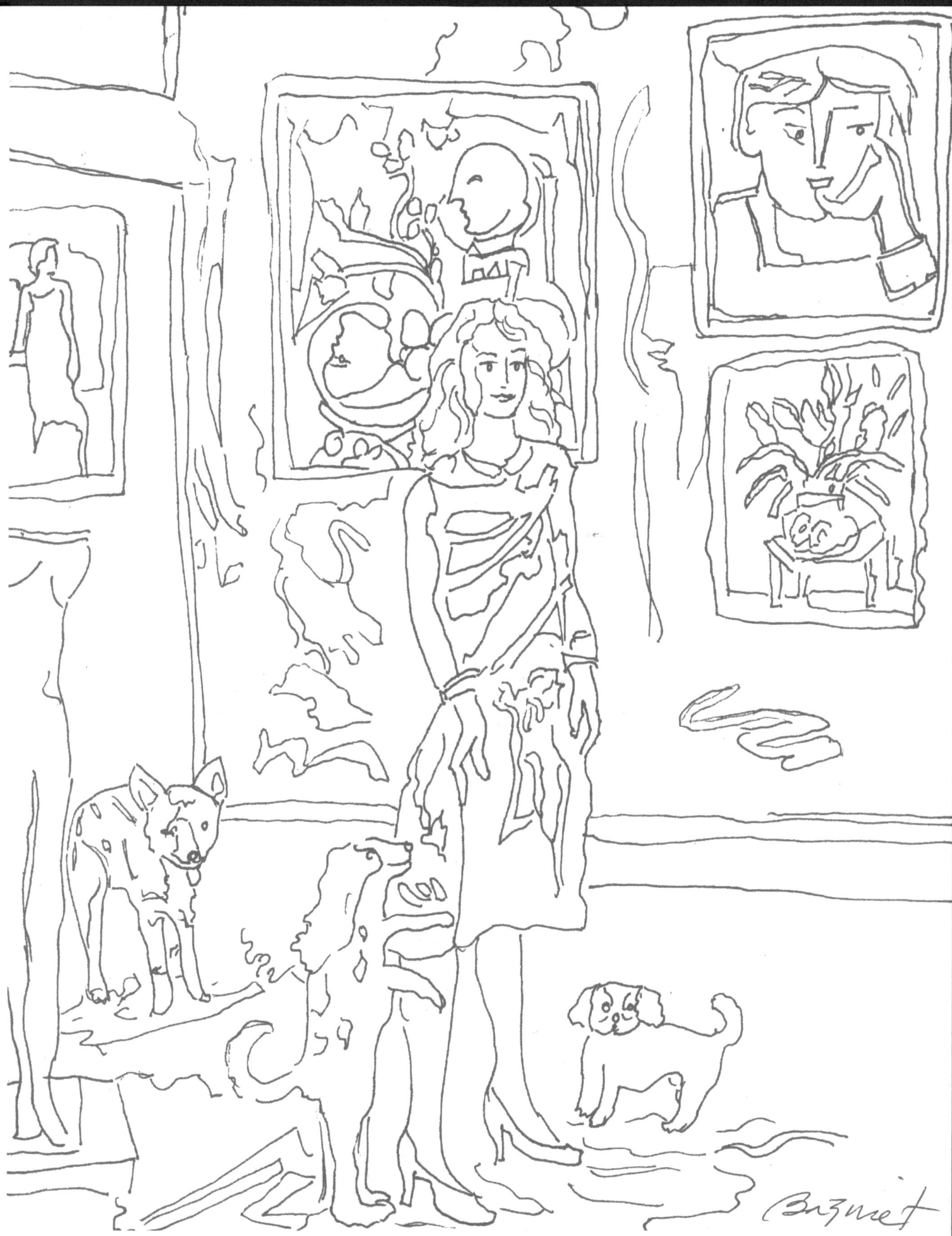

"The Tate Gallery"

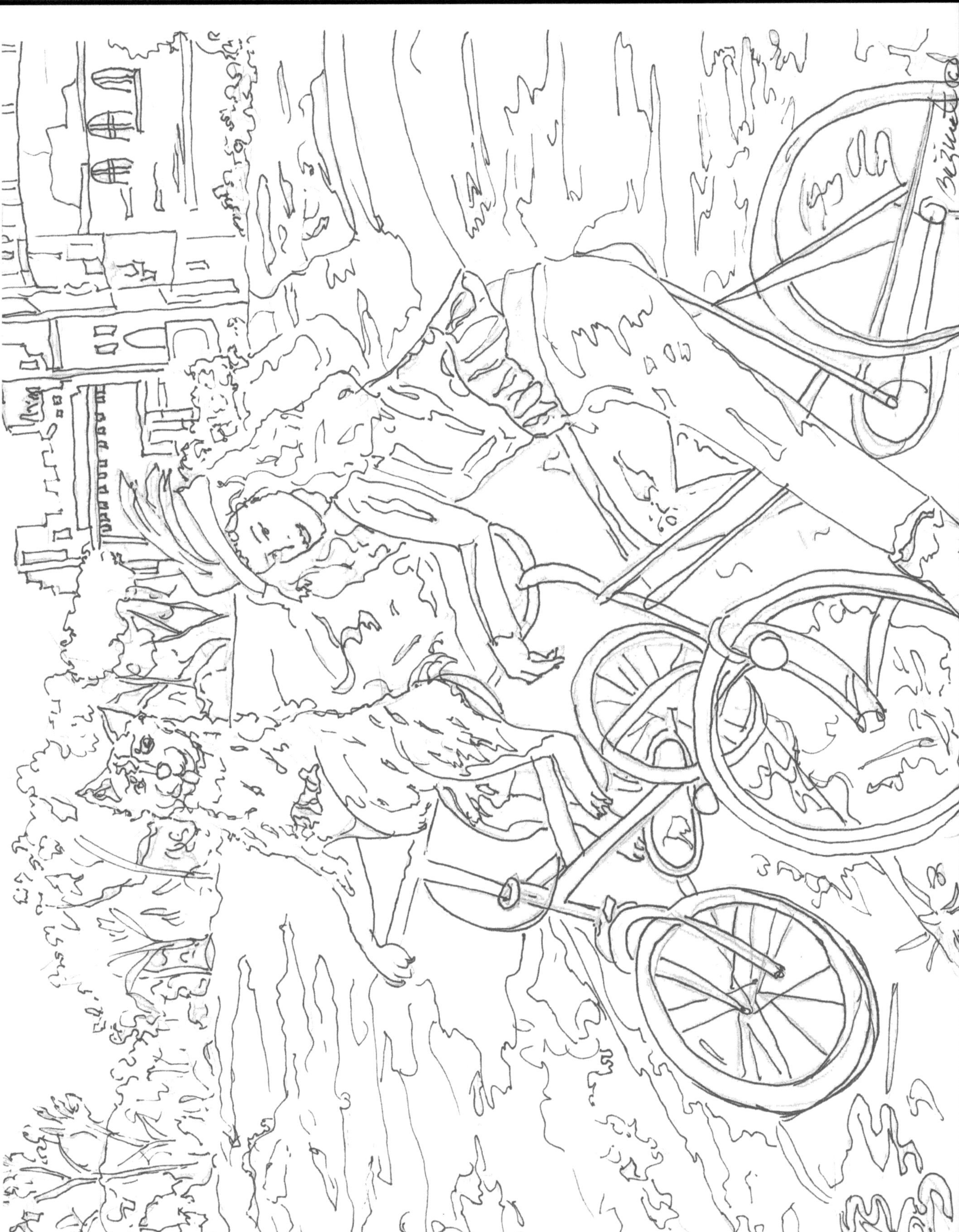

www.ingramcontent.com/pod-product-compliance
Lightning Source LLC
LaVergne TN
LVHW071922110825
818402LV00014B/204